Why Not Me?

Tammy Cranston

(Formerly Tammy Smestad)

TEACH Services, Inc.
P U B L I S H I N G
www.TEACHServices.com • (800) 367-1844

World rights reserved. This book or any portion thereof may not be copied or reproduced in any form or manner whatever, except as provided by law, without the written permission of the publisher, except by a reviewer who may quote brief passages in a review.

The author assumes full responsibility for the accuracy of all facts and quotations as cited in this book. The opinions expressed in this book are the author's personal views and interpretations, and do not necessarily reflect those of the publisher.

This book is provided with the understanding that the publisher is not engaged in giving spiritual, legal, medical, or other professional advice. If authoritative advice is needed, the reader should seek the counsel of a competent professional.

Copyright © 2015 Tammy Cranston

Copyright © 2015 TEACH Services, Inc.

ISBN-13: 978-1-4796-0576-7 (Paperback)

ISBN-13: 978-1-4796-0577-4 (ePub)

ISBN-13: 978-1-4796-0578-1 (Mobi)

Library of Congress Control Number: 2015914983

All Scripture quotations are taken from the Holy Bible, New International Version®, NIV® Copyright ©1973, 1978, 1984, 2011 by Biblica, Inc.® Used by permission. All rights reserved worldwide.

Acknowledgement

First and foremost I want to thank my Lord and Savior for His love, mercy, and grace. I am so thankful for God's goodness. He is worthy of my praise, and my heart's desire is to honor Him with this book.

Through my voice, I have openly shared memories, conversations, and intimate moments to bring glory to God and hope to anyone who currently or has previously experienced a loss in their life. My prayer is that you, the reader, will find inspiration and a desire for a closer walk with God through my story.

While multiple names are included in this story, there is no possible way that I am able to include the names of everyone who prayed, visited, and graciously ministered to Larry and me before, during, and after this journey. To all of you, please know that I am forever grateful! No act of kindness went unnoticed!

Caring Bridge, the website that allows patients with terminal illnesses to keep in touch with loved ones, also deserves recognition. This free online service eased our fatigue and bridged us with family and friends. It is through the comments on Caring Bridge I was able to follow a timeline and personalize my story.

Every manuscript needs to be edited, polished, and refined. For this, I want to thank and commend Elizabeth Nicol, Ruth Carpenter, and my husband, Robert Cranston, for the hours they spent critiquing my manuscript. I gratefully welcomed their input and suggestions.

Lastly, it is appropriate to extend a special thanks to the professional staff at Teach Services, Inc. who made this publication possible.

Contents

	Introduction	7
Chapter 1	Broken Heart and Broken Dreams	8
Chapter 2	Restored Faith	10
Chapter 3	Blessings	15
Chapter 4	Invitations	18
Chapter 5	Permission	22
Chapter 6	Wedding Plans	24
Chapter 7	Memories	27
Chapter 8	Alaskan Cruise	30
Chapter 9	Concerns	32
Chapter 10	Diagnosis	35
Chapter 11	Faced With Decisions	37
Chapter 12	Living Life	39
Chapter 13	Transformation	43
Chapter 14	South Carolina	48
Chapter 15	Returning Home	51
Chapter 16	Birthday Celebration	53
Chapter 17	Humbling Thoughts	55
Chapter 18	Colorado	57
Chapter 19	Surgery	60
Chapter 20	The "Dutchess"	62
Chapter 21	Wyoming	67
Chapter 22	Utah	72
Chapter 23	A Week at Home	76

Chapter 24	**Nashville and the Gulf Shores**	78
Chapter 25	**FedEx Cares**	88
Chapter 26	**Bucket List**	91
Chapter 27	**Testimony**	93
Chapter 28	**Christmas**	95
Chapter 29	**The Sunshine State**	98
Chapter 30	**Hawaiian Cruise**	112
Chapter 31	**Rapid Decline**	119
Chapter 32	**Hospice**	122
Chapter 33	**Last Road Trip**	127
Chapter 34	**World's Coolest Dad**	129
Chapter 35	**Acts of Kindness**	131
Chapter 36	**Unexpected Blessings**	134
Chapter 37	**Too Long**	137
Chapter 38	**Memorial Plans**	142
Chapter 39	**Bringing Larry Home**	146
Chapter 40	**Memorial Service**	148
Chapter 41	**"Caring Bridge" Comments**	159
Chapter 42	**A New Normal**	161
Chapter 43	**Hope and Healing**	165

Introduction

    I felt impressed to write this story because I want others who are alone and hurting to have hope. During my experience I learned that patience and faith are virtues to be developed and exercised. I learned to let God lead, at all times, in all circumstances. He always has my best interest in mind, and He is concerned with the desires of my heart.

    I am grateful God does not give foresight into the future. If He did, I would have said, "No, God, I am not strong enough. I am not ..." I would have had excuses just like Moses did when asked to lead the children of Israel. I now look back with tears of gratitude, knowing God opened doors and led me through them. He was faithful in keeping His promises.

    Christians put their hope in the Lord, not in things of this world. This does not mean Christians are exempt from pain and trials. A life of faith is a prerequisite for a life of hope.

    This book is dedicated to my deceased husband, Larry. I have been told the last three years of Larry's life were the best years of his life. For that, I am grateful. But Larry's best years and my best years will not be on this earth. The best years will be spent in eternity.

Chapter 1

Broken Heart and Broken Dreams

I left work on Friday afternoon as usual, but I felt unusual. I glanced in the mirror and noticed I was driving with a smile, and it felt good. For several years my life had been in turmoil, being tossed to and fro like waves on the sea, but now I was seeing through a different perspective. My marriage of twenty-four years had quickly dissolved. "We have nothing in common anymore" is the explanation my ex-husband, Terry, left me with. He said, "We are not on the same page. We are not even in the same book." I pled with him to attend counseling, but he was not interested. Needless to say, I was emotionally drained.

During the year and a half of our separation, my faith, trust, and relationship with the Lord grew. I was broken and needed mending. I turned to the heart mender Himself for stability and direction in my life. I reached out to Him, and He responded. I felt His love. I felt His grace. I felt His presence. I believed in Him and His Word, but I realized I had not surrendered all. If I had, then why was I carrying so much pain? So all to Jesus ... I surrendered.

Chapter 1 Broken Heart and Broken Dreams

I had a broken heart due to broken dreams. My greatest dream, the desire of my heart, was to be a wife and mother. Family was my driving force, my purpose. My identity was found in these roles. While experiencing personal hurt, I also hurt for my children and future grandchildren. I longed for the family that once was and for the family that could have been. Families are not meant to be broken.

I longed for the family that once was and for the family that could have been. Families are not meant to be broken.

Before the separation, Terry and I discussed selling the house. He assured me we would look for land in the country to build a new home. When our house sold quickly, Terry and I rented a duplex in the small town of Deer Creek. The sale of the house required our oldest son, twenty-two-year-old Travis, to find a new place to call home. At the same time, our seventeen-year-old son Tyler moved into a dorm in preparation for his freshman year of college. Soon after the move to Deer Creek, I was diagnosed with Stage II Melanoma, and three days after my surgery, Terry left. So, within just a few months, my home had been sold, my children had moved, my husband had left, and my health had deteriorated. At that moment I thought this was the most devastating time in my life. Since the last twenty-four years of my life had been devoted to my family, I wondered what I should do next. *How does one start over? How do I find a new normalcy?* I thought.

I had been going to church by myself for quite awhile. My youngest son in college would join me at times, but I would always return home alone. While the stillness and silence were difficult, it was through silence that Jesus ministered to me. While home alone on a particular Friday evening, I cried and prayed. Through my tears, I said, "Dear Lord, you know how devastated I am. My family is gone, and my heart is broken. I have been separated from Terry for a year and a half. The divorce is now final, but my love and my longing for my family to be together does not end simply because a judge signed and stamped a piece of paper. When is it time to let go? What do I do with the rest of my life? I need Your direction, Lord! Can You give me signs, Lord? Signs to let me know if You want me to move forward with my life. I have never asked anything like this before, Lord … but can You give me three signs? Thank You. Thank You, Jesus. Amen."

Chapter 2

Restored Faith

I tossed and turned at night, waking often, as usual. Nights were exceptionally long and hard. In the darkness, in the still of the night, my mind would not rest. Memorizing scripture is what cleared my turbulent thoughts more than anything else I tried. I wrote Bible promises and Bible commands on color-coded index cards. The verses I spent the most time memorizing were the Beatitudes in Matthew 5. I would recite the words I had memorized repetitively until I fell asleep. These words, written in red, Jesus spoke from His own lips:

> Blessed are the poor in spirit, for theirs is the kingdom of heaven. Blessed are those who mourn, for they will be comforted. Blessed are the meek, for they will inherit the earth. Blessed are those who hunger and thirst for righteousness, for they will be filled. Blessed are the merciful, for they will be shown mercy. Blessed are the pure in heart, for they will see God. Blessed are the peacemakers, for they will be called children of God. Blessed are those who are persecuted because of righteousness, for theirs is the kingdom of heaven.

Chapter 2 Restored Faith

When I spoke these words, I pictured Jesus speaking them directly to me. Since this brought me so much comfort, it became my nightly routine. Each week I would study and memorize a new verse. Much to my surprise, within a short time, I had memorized not only the Beatitudes but the entire chapter.

The morning after my heartfelt prayer, I got ready for church and stepped outside onto my covered front porch and listened to the birds sing. It was spectacular! How can this be? How can such tiny creatures sing so melodiously? I smiled on the inside, which in turn, made me smile on the outside. I became accustomed to listening and looking for the "little things" in life. A quote I had previously written in one of my son's scrapbooks said, "Be grateful for the little things in life, for one day, they will become the big things." Some days I was grateful for sunshine or simply watching the squirrels play. But today, I was cherishing the melody of the birds, and I did not want this moment to slip by unappreciated and unnoticed. I was thankful that nature consistently ministered to me. With an attitude of gratitude, my senses seemed to be on overdrive. Being in tune with the intricacies of nature further deepened my relationship with God.

I loved going to church. With my Bible on the empty seat beside me, I placed my key into the ignition of my Ford Explorer, cranked it, and enjoyed the sound of the engine revving. Out of habit, with the intent to lower the volume, I reached for the dial to the CD/radio. Week after week I listened to my favorite Christian CDs on the half-hour drive into town. On this particular Sabbath day though, I made an instantaneous decision to "tune in" to the local Christian radio station. As soon as I heard the first spoken words, the station had my undivided attention. The topic of discussion was biblical reasons for divorce. Of course, the longest discussion was on adultery. But next, the speaker addressed an unbelieving spouse leaving a believing spouse. This topic really hit home with me.

When I heard this message presented by Dr. James Dobson on Focus on the Family, I knew I had received an answer to my prayer. I had just prayed the prayer asking for signs the previous night, so I was amazed to receive an answer so soon. Tears flowed as I felt the release of pain. Why should I be amazed? God is an amazing God! I stored this in my heart and mind, just as the Bible states we should do with God's commandments. Without any doubt, I was absolutely convinced that God had given me my first sign. The verbiage on the radio gave me heart knowledge, as well as head knowledge. I had no control over my ex-husband's decisions. I did have control over my reaction to his decisions, and I decided to trust God. I thanked God for giving me my first sign and for the peace He graciously bestowed upon me.

When I arrived at church, I decided to sit in a pew close to the front on the right side. This was extremely out of the ordinary since I always sat in a back pew on the left. I glanced throughout the room, taking personal inventory of who was in attendance and gave a few nods and smiles. I worship at a small church, so whenever one person is absent, I notice. My thoughts reminded me of the parable of the lost sheep. Ninety-nine sheep are safe under the Shepherd's care, but the Shepherd leaves the ninety-nine to search for the one that is lost. The love and compassion of the Shepherd is such a comforting thought.

I looked forward to hearing Pastor Larry Clonch's sermon. He speaks from the heart, and I always receive a blessing. His sermon this Sabbath day reached down into the depths of my soul. It was so personal I could not control my tears. I felt very relieved to be sitting up front. I hoped, but doubted, the pastor would be the only one in the congregation to notice my uncontrollable tears.

Month after month I carried sorrow and pain. I felt isolated and broken. I joined a Christian support group in order to surround myself with people who could relate to my pain. I signed up for daily inspirational devotions through divorcecare.org. It was comforting to know that someone (even a stranger) understood. I wanted to learn how others put one foot in front of the other to move forward in life. My church family was supportive and kind, but none of them had walked in my shoes. My heavenly Father, who knows my innermost thoughts, knew this message would minister to me.

Previously, during a phone conversation with my sister-in-law she mentioned a verse in Isaiah, "Thy maker shall be thy husband." She said, "Tammy, claim this verse. Jesus can supply all of your needs."

In his sermon, Pastor Clonch spoke of the widow who humbly gave everything she had in her pocket to the Lord. The pastor asked, "Why did she do this? Why did she give everything she had? Because ... Jesus meant everything to her."

She, like me, did not have a husband. She, like me, was alone. Her relationship with the Lord meant everything to her. Jesus fulfilled all of her needs. I knew He would faithfully fulfill my needs as well. I was astonished when Pastor Clonch said, "Please open your Bible to Isaiah 54:5." He proceeded to read, "For your Maker is your husband. The Lord Almighty is his name."

Oh, how I could relate to this verse! I had the reassurance I desperately needed. There was no distance between heaven and my heart. I sought, I asked, and Jesus responded. His love and assurance covered and hovered over me. I knew Jesus had plans for me. My thoughts

Chapter 2 Restored Faith

returned to my prayer, and I realized I had just received my second sign. Amazing grace ... how can it be?

> *There was no distance between heaven and my heart. I sought, I asked, and Jesus responded.*

After church, my best friend, Ellen Bedford, graciously handed me a CD. I could have listened to it on the drive home, but instead, I decided to wait until the afternoon. It was a pleasant thought to have something to look forward to. After lunch I sprawled out comfortably on my bed and gently placed the new CD into the player. I found the music uplifting and inspiring. A message was embedded in each song. The lyrics were strong and clear and the soft melody reminded me of the birds I had heard earlier in the morning. Through the gift of music, I found myself being ministered to again. Once more, I was in tears.

Steve Darmady's song "The Time That Remains" had a powerful message. The lyrics reiterated and reinforced the value of time. The words that so boldly ministered to me talked about lifting Jesus up for others to see, living a life devoted to Him. I was emotionally paralyzed. I still had a meaningful future. It was the unknown causing my fear. I decided to trust God to reveal my future and my purpose. My heavenly Father reassured me He did not want me to live one more moment in vain or in pain.

Some burdens in life can be exceptionally heavy. Uncertainty, pain, and loss were weighing me down. But here, Jesus was telling me, "Cast your cares upon Me." With a grateful, thankful heart, I gave all my cares to Jesus. Guilt, shame, disappointment, and fear were left at His feet. With a lightened heart, I made a firm decision I would not take them back as I had times before.

Jesus had given me my third sign to move forward and not look back. I had pleaded for three signs during my prayer time for a good reason. I did not want any decisions to be derived from my imagination or self-talk. While it seemed time was standing still, it was not. God continued to bless me with the precious gift of time. I was overwhelmed with gratitude. Since words could not express how I felt, my emotional release was to cry. Thankfully, the Lord knew my thoughts! This answered prayer was a milestone or steppingstone in my life, which led me to higher ground.

The prompt answers to my prayer restored my faith. I have read countless stories in the Bible where God spoke, led, and ministered. He spoke directly to Moses at the burning bush. He led the Israelites through the desert. He parted the Red Sea, provided manna for food, and water from a rock. He ministered to Joseph when sold into slavery, to Daniel in the lion's den, to Paul in prison, but now, He personally ministered to me. I had peace like a river, and I could finally say, "It is well, it is well, with my soul." God did not want me to have a troubled heart.

If God is for me, who can be against me? I previously felt empty and timid, with a lack of purpose, but I now realized that God was not done with me. My favorite verse, Jeremiah 29:11, reassured me of this, "'For I know the plans I have for you,' declares the Lord, 'plans to prosper you and not to harm you, plans to give you hope and a future.'" I reminded myself, *God has good intentions for me. Faith, hope, and trust in Him will carry me through. He knows the desires of my heart, my fears, and my longings.*

Where would He lead me? What would He lead me to? I smiled with confidence, knowing my life was in His hands.

Chapter 3

Blessings

Whenever time allowed, my best friend, Ellen, came to visit. Not only did she visit, she faithfully called me every day. Her usual words were, "It's a sister check. How is my sister today?" She always took time to listen, and she often gave me encouraging advice. The support and love I received from her then, and now, is a gift from God. I have been blessed by her friendship. Her compassion and her ministering spirit are contagious. I vowed to reach out to others because of the effect her embrace had on me.

One afternoon while Ellen and I were visiting in my home she shared a story with me about one of her customers. He was a single man, and she considered him a close friend. In fact, she had a relationship with his entire family. She told me the family had four siblings who were all very close. The youngest son, who lived in Oklahoma, had just passed away unexpectedly due to congestive heart failure. Even though they were a Christian family with strong faith, they were now in shock and pain. I told Ellen if she would give me the address of her customer (friend) I would send him a sympathy card. This was in April of 2008.

Ellen knows me well. Not only was she praying for me, she was observing me. She had her eye on me, like God has His eye on the sparrow, and she was assessing my progress every step of the way. It was obvious to Ellen the Lord was moving me forward and I was following His lead. During another visit in May, Ellen felt impressed to ask, "Tammy, would you let me know if or when you would like to meet someone? I have someone in mind I would like to introduce you to." Her facial expressions implied to me that it was a man.

I trust Ellen. I know she, like the Lord, has my best interest in mind. So, of course, I desired to know more. The questions started rolling off my tongue. "What is his name? Where does he live? How old is he? Where does he go to church? How long has he been attending church? What does he look like? What does he do for a living?"

My patient, precious friend proceeded to answer all of my questions. Then she added, "He's compassionate, like you. He wants someone to love, to read the Word of God with, and to pray with." She then pulled her phone out of her pocket. With a smile that lights up a room, she said, "I have a picture of him. Would you like to see it?" As I took her hand in mine, I glanced at the picture and asked her if he knew of me, and she said, "No."

I replayed my conversation with Ellen in my mind long after she was gone. Was I ready for a relationship? Was I ready to open my heart to give love and receive love? Were the scars of trust, love, and loss healed? I prayed about it, and as I often do, I asked God to open doors for me if it was His will, but to close them if it was not. Ellen is a godly woman, and I knew if the Lord impressed upon her heart to introduce us to one another it was God prompting her. After a month of prayer and contemplation, I told Ellen if she still felt impressed to do so, she could make the contact with her friend, Larry. Even though Ellen was not in my presence, I could sense her excitement. She called Larry that very night.

"Hi Larry! How are you?"

Larry said, "I'm fine, but I'm driving in heavy traffic through St. Louis right now, so can I call you back?"

"Of course," Ellen responded. Larry called Ellen back, and she proceeded to ask him if he would be interested in meeting a very special friend of hers. She then told him all about me. She said, "Tammy is about the same size as me (though a little shorter), she has dark hair, she is a good Christian, and she has two adult sons."

Larry said, "Oh, Ellen, I am tired of being hooked up. All my friends keep trying to send me on blind dates, and it just isn't working. Besides, I have been seeing someone from Oklahoma who I feel the Lord wants me to witness to. I need to see where this relationship will go first."

Ellen quickly responded, "OK, Larry. I understand. I'm sorry."

Chapter 3 Blessings

When Ellen shared this information with me, I admit I was disappointed. Afterwards though, I felt relieved, knowing I had prayed about this. For reasons unknown, God was closing this door and that brought me peace. My hope and trust were in the Lord. He was supplying my needs, and neither I nor Ellen desired to interfere in Larry's relationships.

God does work in mysterious ways though. Larry began feeling restless and uncomfortable in his current relationship. He knew the Lord did not want him to get involved in a serious relationship with a non-Christian. Was God closing one door for Larry and opening another? Larry also knew Ellen was a godly woman who would never call about such a matter unless it was taken to the Lord in prayer first. Ellen's call to Larry inspired him to pray more fervently about his future and any God-ordained relationships.

Chapter 4

Invitations

Ellen extended an invitation for me to come to her country home on the weekend since her entire family was gone. She said, "Tammy, I want you to come to the farm and help me with chores. We can even ride the four-wheeler together. We'll have fun!" A weekend getaway sounded appealing to me, so I said "yes" to her bubbly invitation. All throughout my workweek, I looked forward to the upcoming weekend.

Larry had been a FedEx employee for twenty-five years. At this time in his career, Ellen's home was on his designated route. He had a delivery for her on Friday, June 27, 2008. The delivery was a computer, which required a signature. Larry made one attempt to deliver and no one was home, so he returned again in the afternoon before ending his route. The second time around, Ellen was home, and Larry was grateful to make the connection. Larry told Ellen he could not get the name "Tammy" out of his mind. He asked Ellen if she had a picture of me. For some reason, he was thinking he knew me from somewhere. Larry wondered if he knew me from Broadview Academy, the Christian boarding school he attended during his high school years. Ellen was on a mission, searching and searching, shuffling and shuffling, trying to find a picture

Chapter 4 Invitations

of me. Ellen's children and my children had grown up together, and she had many pictures of the children, but none that included me.

Ellen then said to Larry, "She has been my best friend since 1991, but I cannot find a picture of her. I have pictures of our children together, but none with Tammy." She continued, "Tammy is coming to spend the weekend with me, so I will take a picture of her and get it to you."

Larry said, "Better yet. Tomorrow is Mom's birthday, and you are a friend of the family, so why don't you come and celebrate with us and bring Tammy with you?"

Ellen's call to me that afternoon was different from any other call. It wasn't the usual "sister check." She was excited. Before, she was cautious in her role as matchmaker, but now she felt assured that God was leading. She shared with me the open invitation to attend the birthday party at the Smestad home after church on June 28, 2008. At first, I felt apprehensive about meeting someone at a birthday party, but I found comfort in knowing I would be with my best friend and also with fellow church members. Because it was a birthday celebration, I wanted to bring a gift, but not knowing Larry's mother made the decision difficult. I settled on bringing a card and freshly baked peanut butter cookies.

My overnight bag was packed, and I drove directly to Ellen's house after work. Ellen and I did the chores together and then went for a ride on the four-wheeler before retiring for the evening. I went to bed, thanking God for the nice day and the new lease on life. Ellen and I went to church together in Bloomington and came back to her home for a quick lunch before driving into Champaign to attend the birthday party.

Ellen pulled up to the curb of the Smestad home, and though I didn't see Larry, he told me later he had been watching through the large picture window. I opened the passenger door and stepped out into the unknown. Ellen asked me if I was nervous, and with a big smile I simply said, "No." Evidently, Larry was impressed with my smile. Once in the home, I was introduced to Larry, his mother, his father, his sister Ann, from Texas, and his nephew. Time quickly passed with laughter and stimulating conversation. Everyone enjoyed eating cheesecake, which Ann had prepared for the birthday celebration. Unexpectedly, Larry moved over next to me on the couch. He quietly said, "I heard that you like to take walks. Would you be interested in going on a walk with me?" I was more than ready for a break. His family was polite and kind, but I felt a little under the microscope, the only outsider, with all eyes on me.

Larry drove to Parkland, the local community college. He and I walked through their well-maintained gardens. He took me to a pond in which there were very large water lilies. I loved the beautiful pink blooms. This flower has always intrigued me. The lily, with no reasoning capability whatsoever, simply obeys its Creator by opening its bloom in the morning and closing it at dusk. I pondered on the thought of obedience.

Larry and I left the pond from a different location than where we had entered. There was a large step, and because at 5'2" I am a little vertically challenged, I appreciated Larry reaching out to give me a hand. I was impressed by this gesture. During the return walk, Larry and I spoke openly. I asked him questions, and he answered without hesitation. Likewise, I answered any questions he addressed to me. I was very interested in his faith. I wanted to know how long he had been single and how long he had been attending church. When he told me he had been single and attending church regularly for fifteen years, I was relieved. Just because someone attends church, though, does not mean they are serious about their faith. I was eager to learn more about Larry.

Previously, I had written a list of ten attributes I wanted in a significant other. Believing in Jesus and the importance of an ongoing relationship with Him was number one on my list. Valuing marriage, having good morals, enjoying nature, setting goals, and not going to bed angry were additional characteristics on my list. I told God, "These are qualities I would look for in a man, but You know me better than I know myself. If You have someone You are leading me to, please clearly reveal it to me."

While enjoying our casual stroll, Larry and I talked non-stop. Larry was oblivious to the fact that, in my mind, I was checking items off my list. Sometimes Larry would share something, and I would find myself thinking, *That's not on my list, but it's an added bonus.* For example, Larry acknowledged mistakes he had made in the past. He shared how he dealt with the mistake at the time and how he would have handled the situation differently if given a second chance. I appreciated Larry being upfront, and I admired his honesty and sincerity.

Larry and I were not ready to end the walk, but we had been away so long that Ellen called to ask if everything was all right. Larry then drove me back to his parents' home. Ellen and I were preparing to leave since the family had plans to continue celebrating over dinner, but Larry asked if Ellen and I would join them. He was so persuasive that Ellen and I gave in. Dinner was at a Mexican restaurant, El Toro, in Champaign. I do not eat late at night, and I was not hungry, but Larry offered to share just a few bites with me. Larry's family joined hands during prayer. He reached for my hand when the blessing was offered, and I was oblivious to the fact that everyone else was holding hands until after the prayer. I apologized to Larry's nephew, on my right side, for not reaching out for his hand.

It was now getting rather late. Ellen and I needed to leave immediately after returning to the house. Larry stepped out on the front step, gave me a hug, and said, "I want to see you again. I have some business to

Chapter 4 Invitations

take care of the weekend of July 4, but after that I will call you. I promise." He called me on July 5 and told me he was looking forward to seeing me again. He proceeded to share with me the awkward position he was in. He knew that God was leading him to end his developing relationship with his sister-in-law's sister, but to do so required him to see her at a family party, have the tough conversation, and then drive 500 miles with her to Oklahoma to pick up a car he was buying from his sister-in-law that was previously owned by his deceased brother, Rick.

Larry and I began speaking on the phone frequently. The distance from Larry's home in Paxton, Illinois, to my home in Deer Creek, Illinois, was about an hour and a half one way. Ever since the birthday celebration, excluding July 4, Larry and I saw each other every weekend. While making plans one evening, Larry asked me if I would take a road trip with him to Indiana to pick up his car. His red Mazda RX8 had been left behind at his brother's home, so he needed someone to drive with him to Indiana to retrieve it. Larry thought a short road trip would be fun, giving the two of us a chance to get to know each other better. And he was right. Larry's gentle, black pit bull, Buddy, rode along in the back seat.

Larry and I arrived at his brother's home on a hot summer afternoon in the middle of July. After quick introductions to his brother, Brad, and sister-in-law, Deb, everyone changed into swimming suits and jumped into the refreshing pool. Larry and I had an enjoyable day. It didn't take me long to realize his brother, Brad, is a bit of a jokester. On the return trip I drove Larry's new car (previously owned by his brother Rick) with Buddy in the back, while following Larry in the Mazda. The drive took approximately three hours, giving me ample time to think ... particularly about Larry. I was seeing many admirable qualities in Larry. I was especially thankful for shared interests and goals.

> ## *I was seeing many admirable qualities in Larry.*

Larry's birthday was on July 7. I was not with him that weekend, but I wanted to present him with a gift. Several months before meeting Larry, I had a professional photographer take a picture of me. I purchased a nice pewter frame and handed my gift to Larry, hoping he would like it. He loved it! He in turn, gave me a small picture of himself that I placed on the nightstand beside my bed.

Chapter 5

Permission

When my youngest son, Tyler, was home from college for a visit, I told him I wanted to talk with him about something. Since we were sitting on my bed, he had already noticed the picture and as quickly as he pointed to it he said, "I bet that's what you want to talk about." I nodded and said, "yes." I wanted blessings from both of my sons to date Larry since the relationship was quickly progressing. This was an appropriate time for me to ask Tyler, but instead Tyler asked me, "Mom, does he make you happy?"

I said, "Yes."

"Well then, if he makes you happy, he makes me happy," he said.

After Tyler gathered his clean laundry and returned to his dorm, I called my oldest son, Travis, to get his blessings. When asked, Travis responded, "Dad has moved on and is happy. Mom, I want to see you happy too!" Even though I didn't need permission from my adult children, it was encouraging to receive blessings from them.

July and August seemed to fly by faster than usual, primarily because of my new, busy schedule. Larry and I worked hard through the week and looked forward to seeing each other every weekend. A typical weekend included attending church together, long walks with Buddy, and often a country drive on Larry's Harley.

On Sunday, August 31, 2008, I was getting ready to leave Larry's home. As I sat on the floor and reached for my shoes, Buddy quickly sat on them. Larry and I laughed. I was tickled that Buddy did not want me to leave. While walking me to my car, Larry asked if I would like to participate in a motorcycle tour on Labor Day weekend to raise funds for the Muscular Dystrophy Association. "Of course," I said. The event was to take place the following weekend, so Larry completed the registration form immediately after I left.

I was dumbstruck the following Sunday afternoon when Larry and I were sitting on his Harley at the starting point. I had never seen so many motorcycles in one place at the same time. I can recall the sound when the announcer yelled, "Start your bikes." This was a new and exciting experience for me. I met several of Larry's friends who also owned Harleys, and I realized just how loved Larry was. He had a very close relationship with his friends just like he did with his family.

Besides his Harley friends, Larry had many friends related to his FedEx job. He told me how blessed he was to have a job in which he got to see his friends every day. He always greeted his customers with a smile, and over time he became friends with many of them. Often, his customers invited him to weddings, graduation parties, and other celebrations. I was able to attend several of these events with Larry. Larry's customers referred to him as "Larry, the FedEx Man."

Chapter 6

Wedding Plans

    I had a feeling that Larry was going to ask me to marry him someday, but much to my surprise, this happened soon after Labor Day weekend in September. My first instinct was to tell him I thought it was too soon. On the other hand, I knew God had led me to Larry and vice versa. I couldn't think of a good reason to wait, so I boldly answered, "Yes." Obviously, the next big thing was to set a date. Larry and I wanted to avoid the three-hour distance between us during the winter months, so we chose October. With a calendar in hand, the date was quickly narrowed to October 25, 2008. Since this was only two days after my birthday, I jokingly told Larry I would make things easy on him. Next, Larry and I agreed the wedding party would only include family. Friends would be invited only if they were involved in the wedding. One month to plan a wedding is not long, so it was necessary to keep the details very simple.
    Every month Larry used one of his vacation days to create a three-day weekend. It was now the middle of September, and instead of driving to Paxton, Larry drove to my hometown in Deer Creek. On a beautiful Friday afternoon, Larry and I visited the Seventh-day Adventist Church campground, Camp Akita, in Galesburg. The weather was pleasant, and the air had the brisk smell of autumn. The highlight of the camp tour

Chapter 6 Wedding Plans

was riding a 4x4 vehicle over rough terrain. I often felt as if someone was pushing an eject button to throw me out of my seat, but Larry kept me grounded.

Afterwards, Larry and I went shopping in Peoria for my wedding dress. I would come out of the dressing room repeatedly to get Larry's opinion. I wanted the purchase of my dress to be a joint decision. Larry and I decided on a v-neck, off-white gown, which needed to be tailored to properly fit me.

Larry had his eyes on wedding rings long before he asked me to marry him. Often he made deliveries to Hustedt Jewelers, a family owned store in Gibson City. Whenever he entered the store, he looked to see if the wedding rings he had been admiring were still available. I told him I trusted his judgment and gave him permission to make the purchase. During this short time of planning, Larry and I announced the news to family and friends. Larry asked his brother Brad to be his best man, and I asked my best friend, Ellen, to be my matron of honor. After all, God worked through her to bring Larry and me together.

I put in my resignation at my place of employment, and after two long weeks, I was able to dedicate more time to finalizing wedding plans. I also spent time sorting and packing. Larry and I both lived in small homes. I was concerned with combining furniture, dishes, clothing, and all of my pictures! Larry owned a blue antique pickup truck that he used to move my belongings. Two of Larry's closest friends, Billy and Chris, helped with the move. Larry jokingly said, "We are not doing justice to that nice looking truck." He continued, "We look like the Beverly Hillbillies with everything piled on top. All we need is the rocking chair!" I loved Larry's humor.

The fall wedding was beautiful and simple. Taking advantage of fall colors, I had golden yellow, red, and burnt orange mums on the piano. Another fall arrangement cascaded over the wall behind where Larry and I stood. My friend, Penny Matthews, sang, "I Will Be Here" by Steven Curtis Chapman before Larry and I exchanged vows. Penny has a beautiful voice, and I gave her permission to sing whatever song she wanted. Penny later told me she chose this song because of the words about growing older together. Penny said, "I thought this was an appropriate song for a couple getting married later in life."

The lyrics in the song are beautiful, but my favorite line is about the promise we made to each other that day before friends and God. Larry's niece, Lisa, and two other friends took pictures while Tyler videotaped the entire service.

Tyler later presented us with a professional DVD as a gift. After the ceremony, family members joined Larry and me for a celebration dinner at El Toro. For the honeymoon, Larry and I planned an Alaskan cruise the following summer. After the wedding, Larry and I spent the next several months getting acclimated to our Paxton home.

Our wedding day at the Champaign Seventh-day Adventist Church.

Chapter 7

Memories

Knowing I love photography, Larry suggested a photographic road trip. On one of his three-day weekends, Larry and I explored the covered bridges in southern Indiana. Larry stopped at Turkey Run State Park to pick up a map and the quest began to find as many of the covered bridges that we could. It was like being on a scavenger hunt through curvy, country roads. I have treasured pictures of the bridges, but the best treasure was the experience itself.

Larry had no children of his own, so he took special interest in my sons, Travis and Tyler. Often, Travis and his girlfriend, Heather, or Tyler and his girlfriend, Amelia, would join Larry and me for dinner. Travis was working as a tiling contractor, and Tyler was a student at Illinois State University. Larry and I would attend special events at ISU whenever an invitation was extended.

My favorite ISU event was "family day," which was sponsored by the ISU Communication Department. In the production room, Larry, Tyler, and I role-played being news anchors. It was challenging to keep a straight face while being recorded. On purpose, the department supplied humorous scripts with words that were difficult to pronounce. The script was read directly off the teleprompter, so every word was a surprise.

Dining with Travis and Heather.

Tyler, Larry, and Tammy in the TV10 newsroom at Illinois State University on Family Day.

Before leaving, I was handed a DVD, which I cherish and watch whenever I need a good laugh.

On another occasion, Larry and I attended an award ceremony called "The Stewies." Stewies is an abbreviation for Student Television

Workshop Award. Larry and I proudly clapped when the following was announced, "And the winner of best director is awarded to … Tyler Kern." Tyler looked out in the audience and found our smiling faces.

While Tyler was in college, Travis purchased his first home. It was a three-bedroom home with a large yard across from Dee-Mack High School in Mackinaw, Illinois. Travis was in the process of remodeling the entire home. Larry and I enjoyed watching his progress and admired his skills. I was able to help Travis with painting for a few days. He had only one year to work on the home before the bank would do an appraisal. Travis is especially talented in tile work, so his floor to ceiling tiled bathroom is an artistic masterpiece.

The fall months were busy with many birthday celebrations leading right into the holiday and winter season. Larry and I enjoyed every moment spent with family and friends. Celebrating Christmas with the boys and their girlfriends was extra special. Our home was filled with love, joy, and laughter.

During the winter months, Larry and I explored Alaska online. The upcoming Alaskan cruise was a dream vacation. Larry and I wanted to choose excursions and make travel choices that would create lasting memories. The pictures on the Internet were a little foretaste of the magnificent beauty soon to be seen. Even though a balcony room was unbelievably more expensive, Larry and I booked it for the sake of having a breathtaking view at all times. The excursions Larry and I decided on included a seaplane ride in Ketchikan, a Juneau photography tour, including a stop at Mendenhall Glacier, a ride on the most scenic railway of the world in Skagway, and a whale watching tour in British Columbia. What a memorable trip this would be. We eagerly crossed days off the calendar leading up to our honeymoon adventure.

Chapter 8

Alaskan Cruise

On Friday, June 26, 2009, Larry and I flew to Seattle to enjoy the city for a few days before boarding the ship. Larry and I watched the sunset, with a panoramic view, while dining at the Space Needle. The following morning Larry and I excitedly walked the gangway to board the Norwegian Star. After months of anticipation and planning, our honeymoon week had finally arrived!

This was Larry's first cruise and my second. Previously, I had taken a Caribbean cruise with the family when Travis graduated from high school. While I enjoyed the tropical cruise tremendously, I loved the Alaskan cruise just as much. I found the difference between the two cruises as opposite as night is from day. On the Caribbean cruise, crowds gathered around the pool. On the Alaskan cruise, the pool deck was uninhabited and people gathered wherever the ship had windows. For this reason, I was especially thankful Larry and I had booked a private balcony room. The breathtaking view was constant, and neither Larry nor I wanted to miss anything. It wasn't just a view of open seas. The picturesque views included mountains, lighthouses, glaciers, sea lions, seals, whales, and other wildlife.

Chapter 8 Alaskan Cruise

Our honeymoon photo in Alaska on the Norwegian Star.

    The ship first docked at Ketchikan, the gateway to Alaska. After touring the quaint little fishing community in an electric car, Larry and I enjoyed lunch in a second story café, which had a room with a view. After lunch we arrived early at the location of the seaplane ride. I was thankful for the extra time and used it to snap a few pictures. I have a problem with motion sickness, so I hoped I wouldn't regret having lunch before the flight. Unlike Larry, I was apprehensive about flying in a small plane. After boarding, all six passengers were given headphones, which allowed us to listen to soothing music and the pilot telling us about the area. The intent was to enhance excitement and relaxation, and it worked for me!

    Larry and I were sitting in opposite aisles with heads turned outward toward the windows. I took my eyes off the scenery long enough to capture Larry's amazing smile. I knew he was wondering if I was enjoying the ride. When he glanced at me, I communicated with him non-verbally by raising my thumb, and he responded with a nod and a smile. All my anxiety was gone. Flying like a bird, weaving between mountains, and landing in water next to a waterfall was more than spectacular. The seaplane ride was exhilarating, but what I enjoyed the most was seeing Larry so happy.

    Larry and I decided this cruise would be the beginning, the tip of the iceberg, so to speak, of many shared experiences. Often Larry told me he had waited fifteen long years for me. Larry was fulfilling lifelong dreams, and so was I. After this trip Larry spoke more frequently about early retirement, places to travel with me, and adventures to seek.

Chapter 9

Concerns

In April of 2009, three months prior to the Alaskan cruise, Larry had an appointment with his family physician. He decided to see Dr. Sweeney (pseudonym) because he had begun to experience rectal bleeding. I was working full time as a bookkeeper and did not go with him to the appointment. However, Larry told me the doctor said he had a problem with hemorrhoids and advised him to avoid lifting heavy objects. Lifting was a required job responsibility, so I trusted Larry to discuss this matter with his supervisor. I was concerned, but Larry did not seem alarmed, nor did he openly discuss the subject unless I probed him.

In the fall of 2009, after one year of marriage, Larry noticed the bleeding worsening. He left a message with his doctor, who later returned his call. During their phone conversation, Dr. Sweeney suggested that Larry buy hemorrhoidal suppositories. Since I got off work earlier than Larry, he called and asked if I would purchase them for him, which I did. That evening I shared my concerns with Larry and asked if he had ever had a colonoscopy. Larry had had a colonoscopy four years ago, but he also told me he had lost a grandmother to colon cancer, which gave me more reason for concern. The holiday seasons were approaching, which

Chapter 9 Concerns

meant that as a FedEx courier he would be extra busy, but he did promise to seek answers to these growing concerns.

The weeks prior to Christmas are always hectic at FedEx. Unfortunately, during this stressful time, Larry started having abdominal pain. Even though Larry had a demanding schedule, I was thankful he called Dr. Sweeney to schedule an appointment. Due to her medical school teaching schedule, she was unavailable in December, but Larry did get an appointment scheduled for early January. At this appointment Dr. Sweeney voiced concerns about a possible hernia. A CAT scan was ordered and scheduled on February 19, 2010.

Larry and I were enjoying dinner on Sunday afternoon in Bloomington with Tyler and his girlfriend, Amelia, when Larry received a phone call from the doctor. Dr. Sweeney said, "I have your results. The CAT scan shows that you do have two small hernias, but I am more concerned with the spots on your liver." Larry was not expecting to hear these words. He asked Dr. Sweeney if this could be cancer. The doctor replied, "We will have to do more tests to find out."

Larry had an MRI on March 12, 2010, in which he was told the spots looked larger and there were more of them. On April 8, 2010, a year after his first symptoms, Larry had a PET scan. The results of the procedure showed Larry's entire liver glowing. The concerns and fears each step of the way now weighed heavier and heavier on us. In the meantime, before Dr. Sweeney even suggested it, Larry and I scheduled a colonoscopy.

On April 16, 2010, a colonoscopy was attempted, but the procedure was prematurely halted due to a blockage by a mass lesion. The surgeon took a biopsy and told us to expect results the following Monday morning. By all appearances, the PET scan and lesion in the colon were pointing to the diagnosis of cancer.

It seemed as if the doctor, even prior to the pathology results, was telling us that devastating news would be coming soon enough.

Prior to the colonoscopy, we had planned a weekend trip to Michigan to visit Larry's niece and her family of six. Larry and I loved spending time with this family. They are a family that prays together and plays together. Because of the circumstances, I said to the doctor, "Maybe we should cancel this weekend trip."

The surgeon replied, "No, I think you should go and be with family." It seemed as if the doctor, even prior to the pathology results, was telling us that devastating news would be coming soon enough. He wanted us to enjoy time with family.

Larry and I took the weekend trip to Michigan, but it was different from any other road trip. Rightly so, most of the conversation was about Larry's appointments, results, and awaiting diagnosis. It was a blessing to be with family though, and the children unknowingly helped soothe and divert our troubled hearts. The change of pace was refreshing. Larry and I enjoyed attending the worship service in Berrien Springs with the family. Lisa, Larry's niece, prepared lasagna for lunch after church.

Cancer constantly lurked on my shoulder, desiring to take up residence in my heart and mind, and I was unwelcoming. Again, I heard Christ lovingly say, "Cast your cares upon Me." I could not and would not get through this on my own. I did, however, question the Lord's timing. Why would this happen after just one year together? I wondered how Larry would handle hearing a devastating diagnosis on Monday morning—I wondered how I would handle it.

Oh, how Larry and I need you, Lord! I prayed.

Chapter 10

Diagnosis

There are moments in time forever etched in my memory. Monday, April 19, 2010, precisely at 8:00 a.m., is one of those moments. Larry and I were standing in one of Dr. Sweeney's examination rooms. The doctor, who was also standing, said, "I have your results and it is not good." I noticed her demeanor. She seemed cold. She spoke so matter-of-factly. I did not sense any empathy whatsoever as she continued. "You have stage IV cancer." She then proceeded to hand over the pathology report.

I thought I was prepared to hear "cancer," but I was not. Especially, not stage IV. I did not feel steady on my feet as my eyes scanned the pathology report. I wanted to see the pathologist confirmation more than I wanted to hear the doctor speak. I was having trouble locating what I was searching for, so I finally said, "I don't see anywhere on the report where it says stage IV cancer."

Dr. Sweeney said, "Larry has colon cancer with metastatic disease to the liver and that automatically makes it stage IV cancer."

What is he thinking?

I glanced at Larry who was showing no emotion at all. *What is he feeling? What is he thinking?* I wondered.

Dr. Sweeney said, "I would like for you to meet with an oncologist. Can I set up an appointment for you?"

All eyes were on Larry since the question was directed to him. He confidently replied, "No. I do not want to go through radiation or chemotherapy. I want to enjoy whatever time I have left."

Dr. Sweeney shocked both of us when she said, "I don't blame you. If I was in your shoes, I wouldn't either."

While maintaining his composure, Larry asked, "How much time do you think I have?"

Dr. Sweeney most likely quoted directly from a medical journal as she answered, "If you have chemotherapy, maybe three years at most, if you do not, less than one year."

I thought to myself, *She is not God. She is quoting statistics.* Larry was ready to walk out the door, and I followed his lead. Larry had heard enough and so had I. It was time for Larry and me, as a couple, to partner with God in regard to this news.

Anticipating the diagnosis and hearing the pathology report was hard, but Larry and I both knew the days ahead would be harder. It was now time for us to learn to live with cancer. It was also time to face the possibility of death. Even though Larry was the one with the terminal diagnosis, I felt a part of myself dying as well. Only God would sustain both of us.

I knew Larry did not want to see an oncologist to pursue chemotherapy or radiation therapy, and I supported his decision. The topic had previously been discussed, so it was unproductive to bring it up again. We both felt strongly, however, that doing something would be better than doing nothing. As Larry and I walked, hand in hand, to the car, with tears, I said, "Larry, what's next?" We worked through a lengthy conversation, covering everything from seeking a second opinion, to just living life, or to possibly seeking alternative treatments. The hours of conversation were emotionally and physically exhausting. Phone calls to family and friends added to the fatigue.

Larry and I were carrying a heavy load, and we both knew what to do with it. What could we do, but pray. Pray continually. Pray fervently. I recalled how the Lord had graciously answered my prayers in the past. I knew the Lord could heal Larry if it was His will. But what if it was not? My mind often wandered through the "what ifs ..." Day after day, the Lord ministered to my troubled soul. He reminded me to live in the moment.

Chapter 11

Faced With Decisions

Larry was known for being a fun, outgoing man, but in regards to his feelings, he was very reserved. This is why I was not expecting to hear the following words Larry spoke. Soon after the diagnosis, Larry said, "I have always wanted to be a witness for the Lord, but I never knew the words to say. I never felt comfortable approaching someone one on one. This is my chance to be a witness." I agreed with Larry, and as a couple, we prayed for open doors. Devastating news like this happens every day to other people, but now it was personal. Family and friends were watching us closely. Larry and I were under careful scrutiny here on earth, and all of heaven was watching as well.

Family and friends were watching us closely. Larry and I were under careful scrutiny here on earth, and all of heaven was watching as well.

A joint decision was made to visit Mayo Clinic in Rochester, Minnesota. During a phone conversation, surgery to remove the lesion in Larry's colon and a possible liver dissection was discussed. Larry's appointment was on May 6, 2010, just one day prior to Tyler's college graduation. Larry did not want to miss the graduation, nor did I. Mayo Clinic, however, generously agreed to see Larry quickly, so the date and time were non-negotiable.

I felt that I had to be at this appointment with my husband. Under the assumption that Larry would be admitted to Mayo, plans were made for me to stay with Larry as long as possible but still rush down to Normal to attend Tyler's graduation. I would stay with Larry during his CAT scan and lab work on Thursday and as long as possible during his two appointments on Friday. I would then drive to Tyler's graduation and return to Minnesota the following day.

During Larry's first appointment on Friday, he and I met with two oncologists who confirmed the stage IV cancer diagnosis. Unlike Dr. Sweeney, the doctors compassionately discussed Larry's illness and said, "We cannot perform the surgery on your liver until you go through chemotherapy. The lesions are just too large, and there are too many of them. We need to try to shrink them first. We can repeat the CAT scan in two months."

With no hesitation, Larry again said "no" to chemotherapy. The oncologists insistently gave Larry another treatment option. The team suggested radiofrequency ablation, which they stated would most likely buy him more time. Knowing I should have left for the graduation hours ago, Larry said, "I only came here because I was interested in surgery. I sincerely thank you for your time, but I need to leave." Larry and I walked out the door, and he quickly asked me, "Can you wait for me to pack my bag? I want to go with you."

Chapter 12

Living Life

I worried that going back to the hotel and waiting for Larry to pack his bags would make us late. I should have been on the road an hour and a half earlier. Tyler was expecting me though, not Larry. What a surprise it would be for him to see Larry! I had arranged a meeting place with Tyler where I would take pictures of him before the ceremony. Due to the time constraint, I realized I would not see Tyler before graduation, nor get pictures. Regardless, Tyler would be happy, and Larry was overflowing with joy. Larry did not want to miss this once in a lifetime opportunity. He was focused on living life, and cancer and surgery were no longer on his mind.

The drive from Rochester to Normal, Illinois, normally takes almost ten hours. Larry insisted on driving, and I knew why. He felt more comfortable pushing the speed limit, and he was on a mission. I was astonished at how quickly the trip went. After finding a parking space, Larry and I walked to the pre-arranged meeting place. I did not see Tyler, but decided to wait at that spot for just a few more minutes. I glanced down the sidewalk and saw Tyler casually walking with his dad. When the distance closed in, he began running. Tyler had spotted Larry, and he could not believe he was there. Like a movie playing in slow motion, Tyler ran and wrapped his arms around Larry and said, "I wasn't expecting you."

Larry said, "I didn't want to miss it." I explained the late start to Tyler and expressed how surprised I was to have made it on time. Tyler looked at Larry and said, "Who are you? Superman?"

May 7, 2010, was a good day, and I did get outstanding pictures. Pictures that included Larry!

Tyler greeting Larry—it was a great surprise!

Tammy, Tyler, and Larry at Tyler's college graduation ceremony.

Chapter 12 Living Life

Moments like the graduation ceremony relieved my mind for a few hours. I longed for more moments like this. What would the summer bring? Would Larry be present in the fall or better yet, would he be here for Christmas? Was one year or less all that would be left? The value of time was constantly on my mind. Time was a precious commodity. I recalled the lyrics to the song "The Time that Remains" that God had used to reassure me that I should move forward with my life.

Larry and I loved planning outings and writing them on the calendar. Either Larry or I would often say, "One week, or two weeks before we go to …" Prior to Larry's diagnosis, we had planned two vacations. In June we planned to drive to South Carolina to stay in a lake house owned by my former boss, Rhonda. In July we were scheduled to vacation with his sister, Ann, and her husband, Don, in Pagosa Springs, Colorado. Larry was feeling relatively well except for some minor pain in his abdomen, so the scheduled vacations remained on the calendar.

After Larry's diagnosis in April, he never returned to work. Larry and I met with his supervisor, Ken, for instructions on completing the disability paperwork. In addition to Larry's health insurance and disability insurance, he owned a life insurance policy through FedEx. At this meeting, Ken asked, "Did you know that with a terminal illness you can cash up to 50 percent of your life insurance?"

Neither Larry nor I had any knowledge of this. Larry was planning on retiring in just two years, and his dream was to buy a motor home and travel. Instantaneously, Larry and I had the same thought, confirmed through our smiles. The advancement would give us the opportunity he longed for. Larry gratefully asked for the application.

Prior to his diagnosis, we had attended motor home shows. In fact, I had started a file on the brochures and pamphlets he had collected. With the possibility of purchasing a motor home on the horizon, the gloom of death was lifted from Larry, and with renewed zeal he looked forward to tomorrow and the day after. Immediately, just like I knew he would, Larry began searching for a suitable motor home. It was good to see him focused and active.

In regards to the cancer, however, Larry and I still felt compelled to do something. The Seventh-day Adventist Church has alternative wellness centers throughout the country. Larry and I researched them online and agreed that Eden Valley in Colorado would be our best option. Larry prayed before calling, asking God to open the door if this is where He was leading. When an employee from Eden Valley answered, they informed us that they had a full schedule until mid-July. The staff prayed with us over the phone and said they would keep his name on a waiting list.

Uchee Pines in Alabama was the second wellness center that interested Larry. No one answered when Larry called, so he left a detailed message. When a staff member returned the phone call, we were informed the facility took no more than twelve patients at a time. For the upcoming session, they currently had eleven spots reserved. Larry and I looked at each other and knew this was an answer to prayer, an open door. The staff member said, "Why don't you pray about it and call back?" There was no need to pray.

Larry said to the man, "The remaining opening is an answer to prayer. Please put my name on the list." The session was scheduled to begin the following Sunday. Larry and I would arrive at their facility on May 16, 2010, and be discharged on June 2, 2010.

Larry and I were confident in God's providence. We reveled in His word.

The staff member on the phone explained the natural cancer treatments provided at their facility, including an infrared sauna (light), hyperbaric chamber (oxygen), and hydrotherapy (hot baths). They also had a Wellness Pro machine with frequencies that neutralize cancer cells through an electric charge. And of course, Larry would be eating a lot of greens and would continue the raw juicing he had already been doing at home. Larry was a little apprehensive about the hydrotherapy treatment in which his core body temperature would be raised to 104–106 degrees for about twenty minutes.

But our concerns were diminished because we knew God had opened the right door at the right time. Larry and I were confident in God's providence. We reveled in His word, "Ask and it will be given to you; seek and you will find; knock and the door will be opened to you" (Luke 11:9, 10).

Chapter 13

Transformation

Larry and I quickly packed for the two-week stay in Alabama, which we would follow with the planned vacation to South Carolina immediately afterwards. Two days after the phone call to Uchee Pines, Larry and I were on the road. When we arrived at the facility in Seale, Alabama, I commented on how beautiful the setting was. It was not like a hospital or hotel, but more like a retreat center. The facility was a one-story brick building with many windows and patios. Surrounding the building were gorgeous pine trees and several hiking trails. Once inside, I was pleased with the private bedroom and bathroom, which would be home away from home for the next two weeks.

Both Larry and I were exhausted from talking on the phone so often to so many family and friends. Thankfully, my former employer told me about a website called Caring Bridge. The user-friendly website is available free of charge to anyone who has a terminal illness. The purpose of the website is to stay in touch with family and friends through blog postings. The patient, or a family member, writes updated messages in a journal, which I handled for Larry. Family and friends view the journal and post messages in the guestbook if they desire to do so. This was such a blessing, since everyone wanted to keep in touch and be informed. I took the time to set up the webpage prior to leaving for Uchee Pines.

In the evening, the staff at Uchee Pines allotted time for the patients and families to get acquainted through a spiritual and informational meeting. It was nice to meet the other eleven patients and the staff and learn about the very structured schedule. Each patient at Uchee Pines was assigned a counselor. Out of twelve patients, Larry was the only male and was, therefore, assigned three counselors to work with him—Calwyn, Martin, and Sean. Larry loved joking with them and often referred to them as his three amigos, since they followed him everywhere.

One day while Larry was having a hydrotherapy treatment, I asked Calwyn if I could borrow his computer to update Larry's journal on Caring Bridge. While Larry was boiling in the 105-degree water with ice on his head, I read to him what I had written. I then asked him if he had anything he wanted to add. His reply was, "Yes, say it is hot here in Alabama!" That was Larry, a man of few words.

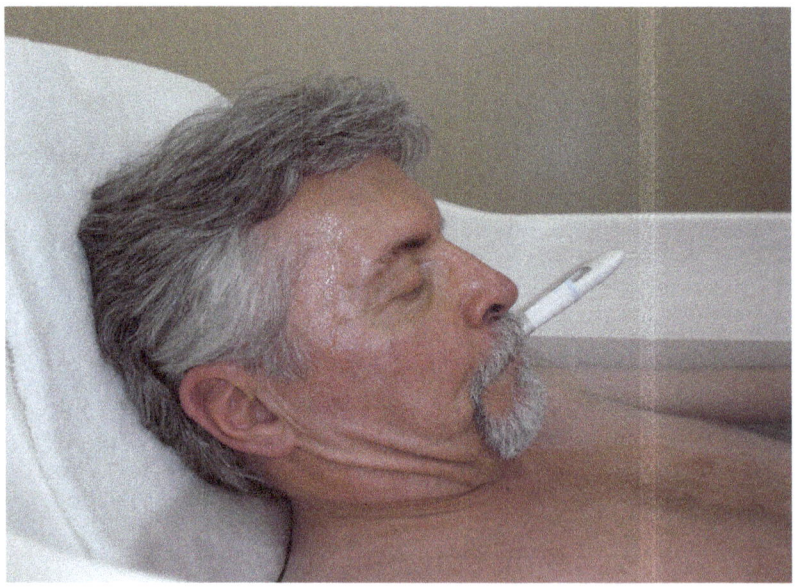

Larry's hydrotherapy treatment—the goal was to elevate the core body temperature to 105 degrees.

I was at Larry's side during every treatment. I have to admit the hydrotherapy treatment, in particular, looked very uncomfortable. After the treatment, the staff wrapped Larry up like a mummy, and he was instructed to lie flat on his bed for an hour while he continued to sweat and keep his temperature up. His perseverance amazed me. I knew Jesus was providing Larry sufficient strength for each day.

Chapter 13 Transformation

Larry and I had a consultation with Dr. Killman Boutet, one of the two doctors on staff at the facility. When Larry met Dr. Boutet for the first time, he commented on his first name. He jokingly said, "This is wrong. No doctor should have the name 'kill man'." Dr. Boutet laughed and then patiently answered questions and reviewed Larry's lab work. Larry was informed that his blood work showed problems with his kidneys and borderline diabetes. The doctor used this information to make changes in Larry's treatment plan.

On May 24, 2010, I posted the following message on Larry's Caring Bridge website:

> Hello, everyone! I just finished reading the comments in the guestbook to Larry. He enjoyed them very much. He likes to hear what is going on with you. As you know, he is in his second week at Uchee Pines. He is handling his hydrotherapy treatments better, although he did receive a break over the weekend. After his treatment today, he will have an infrared dome placed over his abdomen. He was very happy about lunch today. He actually had spaghetti with meatballs, meatless of course. It was a nice change since he has been having beans and salads twice a day. He just has fruit to eat in the evening.
>
> He is having difficulty drinking everything they want him to drink as it doesn't taste well and it fills him up. They originally put him on a tea (that I make) that has around eight herbs in it that Larry says smells like the lawn mower after he's mowed. Also, he drinks an eight-ounce glass of water with charcoal, along with aloe vera and chia seeds. They recently added lemons to his diet, and this is very hard for him to get down at times. He will be seeing the doctor this afternoon, and I will update you on what he says.
>
> Larry and I are learning so much information in the classes here that we can't wait to share. For the last three evenings, Dr. Diane has been sharing her testimony with us. She is one of the doctors here and her only daughter died at a young age from leukemia. I read this to Larry and asked him if there was anything he wanted to add and he said, "Yes! Send for help!" He has made a lot of changes, but the one thing that hasn't changed is his humor! Thanks for your prayers and God bless!

As hard as this was at times for Larry, overall he was pleased to be at Uchee Pines. The spiritual atmosphere was uplifting to him, and to me as well. Patients and staff partnered together in worship, devotions, and prayer. Uchee Pines has a very large organic garden, and Larry and

I became acquainted with the gardener and his family. All patients were encouraged to take walks in the fresh air at least twice a day. Larry and I walked around the large garden or often walked the hiking trails, enjoying the aroma of the many pine trees.

Larry showcasing a pine cone on the hiking trail at Uchee Pines.

    On our last Friday afternoon, Larry and I drove into town to purchase some needed supplies. Calwyn asked for permission to ride along since he did not own a car. Almost all of the staff working at Uchee Pines live close enough to either walk or ride a bicycle to work. No wonder they look so healthy! Driving into town was a bit discouraging for us. Signs were posted everywhere advertising fast food and many other unhealthy tempting options. Larry and I had become accustomed to the simple lifestyle Uchee Pines provided. The lifestyle center was a safe haven, secluded from worldly distractions.

    Before departing Uchee Pines, I was offered an opportunity to receive a hydrotherapy treatment. I agreed in order to experience firsthand what Larry had been going through. I found out that by no means is this a spa treatment. One time was enough for me! After experiencing

Chapter 13 Transformation

this myself, I was thoroughly amazed at Larry's attitude. How could he never utter a complaint?

In my opinion, the contrast bath looked more uncomfortable than the hydrotherapy treatment. The contrast bath consisted of three minutes in hot water and thirty seconds in cold. Larry stepped side by side into each tub. The cold tub literally had ice cubes floating in it. The staff said patients usually alternate between the two tubs seven times, but Larry wanted to make it worth his while so he repeatedly did this ten times. I think Larry took pride in the fact that he was doing something to fight his cancer. I was extremely proud of him.

The day before leaving Uchee Pines, Larry had a final appointment with the doctor to review his lab work again. During the two-week period, Larry's liver function had deteriorated, but there was major improvement with his cholesterol and parasites counts. Hugs and tears were exchanged while Larry and I said goodbye to the staff and remaining patients. Before leaving, the kitchen staff handed us a healthy lunch packed out of love.

On June 2, 2010, Larry and I reverently drove around the organic garden and facility one last time. I was appreciative of the transformation I had seen in Larry. He had come with cancer and was leaving with cancer, but a heart transplant had taken place. His relationship with the Lord had been strengthened. As hard as it was to leave, Larry and I were excited about vacationing in South Carolina. One thing I would not miss was the 5:45 a.m. wake-up bell.

Chapter 14

South Carolina

    Larry was a pleasant travel companion. He was determined to create good memories with me. I found Larry's excitement contagious, and I was so thankful for his patience. He usually drove but would stop whenever I wanted to take a picture. It was nice to be on the road again with him. The drive gave us time for discussion and reflection. Within a short time, we arrived at the gated property in West Union, South Carolina, which overlooked a large, beautiful lake.

    The cottage house located in Backwater Landing was a perfect vacation retreat for us. On the backside of the home was a covered, screened porch overlooking Lake Keowee. While standing in front of the home, mountains could be seen in the distance. Rhonda, my former employer and owner of the home, had informed us about the many waterfalls close by. In fact, she said there were twenty waterfalls within an hour distance from the home.

    When daylight broke, Larry and I purchased a map and the waterfall exploration began. While driving and searching, I recalled the covered bridge exploration in Indiana. During the week, Larry and I found ten waterfalls, some off the beaten path, deep in the woods. Each waterfall was unique and breathtaking! At one waterfall Larry and I were actually

Chapter 14 South Carolina

able to walk underneath while the water cascaded loudly in front. The most breathtaking, massive, and beautiful was Whitewater Falls located on the border of North and South Carolina. The waterfall drops over 1,071 feet and is the highest falls east of the Rocky Mountains.

Larry and Tammy at Whitewater Falls on the border of North and South Carolina.

Larry and I had never been to the beach as a couple, so we planned a day's excursion to Myrtle Beach. The drive was long but well worth it. As soon as Larry's feet touched the sand, he started searching for seashells. I realized this was exactly where Larry needed to be. Being in nature, exploring waterfalls, or walking the beach brought peace, comfort, and joy to Larry's heart and to mine as well. In moments like that, for short periods, cancer did not exist.

After Tyler's college graduation, he moved to Nashville, Tennessee. Larry and I decided to drive the scenic route on the return trip, through the Smoky Mountains, to visit Tyler and his girlfriend. Amelia had to work the following morning so Tyler, Larry, and I drove her to her place of employment in downtown Nashville. The downtown area was booming with live events, so the three of us decided to walk around for a while. Tyler noticed a competition called, "The Singing Bee," which he hesitantly decided to enter. During the game music plays (country, of course), but when the music stops, the contestant must continue singing the lyrics. Whoever does the best, after several rounds, is placed on a waiting list for the game show that is aired nationally on the Country Music Television Station (CMT). Tyler was doing rather well until a young girl, a big fan of Taylor Swift, knew every lyric of an entire song. We all smiled and laughed during this competition, but the biggest blessing was watching Larry lose himself in a lighthearted moment.

Larry savored moments, and so did I. I now had a better understanding of what cancer could not do.

By Larry's side I was able to witness firsthand how a cheerful heart is good medicine. Larry savored moments, and so did I. I now had a better understanding of what cancer could not do. Cancer could not rob us of love. Cancer could not shatter our hopes, dreams, and faith. When Larry and I traveled and explored God's creation, we felt so alive. Is this why it felt so bittersweet to return home from our month-long journey?

Chapter 15

Returning Home

On June 21, 2010, Larry and I returned home after being away for more than a month. Margaret, a close friend and neighbor, who had been checking on the home, left mail on the kitchen counter that she had graciously gathered. Larry and I looked forward to interacting again with family and friends, like Gary and Margaret. This was the advantage of returning home. However, the disadvantage was facing the reality of cancer. At home we could not escape discussing cancer with family and friends. At home cancer controlled our schedule with doctor's visits and tests.

Larry desired to have some sort of routine for the next few months. Since I had been trained on giving Larry hydrotherapy treatments, he wanted to continue this practice. Close friends from church had a hot tub that would heat to 110 degrees. The couple allowed Larry to use the hot tub at our convenience. While at Uchee Pines, Larry also received hyperbaric oxygen treatments, and he remembered a close friend and customer who owned a hyperbaric chamber. She was trained on using this machine to treat her son who had frequent seizures. Larry called Linda who willingly offered to give him treatments. In addition, Larry received periodic infrared sauna treatments at another friend's home. Larry felt exceptionally blessed to have the opportunity to continue the treatments he was accustomed to.

    For thirteen weeks, Larry and I had been waiting to receive a disability check. Thankfully, it finally arrived. Larry was on short-term disability for ninety days. Before he could get approval for long-term disability, it was mandatory for him to file for social security benefits. "I will take care of this," I said to myself, "but not now." Larry's birthday was fast approaching on July 7, so my first priority was to plan a birthday party.

Chapter 16

Birthday Celebration

    The party was held at Larry's parents home in Champaign on Sunday afternoon. The party was a family reunion with Larry at the center of attention. Many of Larry's family members were present. Larry's niece and her family of six from Michigan were there. Larry's brother, Brad, from Indiana and his sister, Ann, from Texas were also present as well as many nieces and nephews.

    The last time this entire group had been together was for a joyful event, our wedding day. Now Larry's loved ones gathered together to celebrate his birthday. Cancer was an uninvited guest to this family celebration. Everyone wanted to have their pictures taken with Larry, well aware that this might be their last opportunity to do so.

    Photography is a passion of mine. I find great joy in taking pictures and preserving memories. I've heard the cliché that pictures are worth a thousand words. In the future, what would my pictures say about Larry? Instead of cancer, would they tell a story about faith, love, and joy?

    Larry truly enjoyed having his family members together. He grinned ear to ear when he was able to take his young niece for a ride on his motorcycle. If the doctors were right, this would be Larry's last birthday.

Larry's nieces, nephews, brother (Brad), sister (Ann), and parents (Blair and Lois) at his birthday celebration.

What a day of mixed joy and sorrow. Happiness radiated outwardly, while sadness was constrained to the heart. Again, my mind wandered to the "what ifs" and the returning question, "How long, Lord?" The road Larry and I were traveling was long and hard, with no escape from the underlying concerns. Thankfully, God was posting signs and providing light amidst the darkness.

Chapter 17

Humbling Thoughts

I cannot survive without breathing, nor will I survive without putting all of my trust in the Lord. I learned to embrace life and love with no regrets. Love hurts and love heals. Like Larry, I did not want a pity party. Instead, I focused on all that was good. I thanked God for bringing Larry into my life. It is a humbling thought to think that God chose me to walk this journey with Larry. What a privilege and an honor! Faith, trust, and love are virtues strengthened through trials like this. Larry's perseverance additionally gave me strength as his health continued to deteriorate.

On Monday, July 26, 2010, a few weeks after Larry's birthday, he had a routine doctor's appointment. As always, lab work was drawn. Previously, Larry's CEA test (a marker of cancer activity) was 5.0, but now it had elevated to 8.0. Larry's oncologist also scheduled another CAT scan for the middle of August. At all these appointments, Larry heard the same negative results as I did, but he never dwelt on them. He focused on living.

For my own sanity, I had to, at times, think about how my life would be after losing Larry. Death meant living the rest of my life without him. Death meant walking faithfully beside my husband while he slowly declined. Death meant being strong enough to watch Larry take his final breath. Death meant finding new meaning and a new purpose for my life.

All these thoughts were overwhelming. What could I do, except pray? I prayed consistently and fervently for the Lord to carry us through this journey.

For my own sanity, I had to, at times, think about how my life would be after losing Larry.

Larry and I were actively experiencing grief. While among the living, Larry was grieving. He was experiencing preparatory grief. He was dealing with his illness, his loss of independence, and his shortened time with loved ones. On the other hand, I was experiencing anticipatory grief with thoughts of losing him. Throughout this whole process, I was very in tune with my thoughts and feelings, hoping that someday I could help others through their unique grieving experiences.

Chapter 18

Colorado

Larry and I joyfully looked forward to vacationing in Pagosa Springs, Colorado. Larry was still feeling rather well, but he did have some bad days with minor pain in his abdomen. Regardless, we were excited about hiking and exploring God's creation. Larry and I purchased brand new hiking boots and began breaking them in by wearing them on short walks around the neighborhood. This vacation would be a memorable time with family. Larry's sister, Ann, brother-in-law, Don, their adult son, Nathan, and pet dog, Bandit, would be with us the entire week.

We arrived in Colorado early enough in the day to take a short hike with Ann. Unfortunately, the first day ended in the emergency room. Larry fell backwards down a ravine. Collectively, we had decided to take a short cut and cross a ravine. It was not exceptionally steep, but there was a lot of loose dirt, which made it hard to keep your footing. Larry had noticed a dead root protruding out of the ground so he grabbed it while he turned himself around in order to walk down the hill backwards, hoping for better traction. Ann and I heard the root snap, and as quickly as we heard it we watched Larry do a backwards somersault down the ravine. Ann quickly slid down the hill while I was ready to run for help since we did not have our cell phones with us. I yelled out to Larry, "Are you alright? Do I need to call 911?"

Larry, Tammy, Ann, Don, (Bandit on leash), and Nathan at the Continental Divide Trail in Colorado.

Larry said, "Give me a minute. Give me a minute." He decided to stand up although he could not stand up straight. He walked hunched over until he could get out of the ravine in an area of the hillside that was not as steep.

Why did this happen to Larry? Why couldn't it have been me? I thought.

Even though Larry was extremely sore, he was up and moving within several days. Ann is a physical therapist, and she proved to be very helpful with nursing Larry. She used massage therapy and stretching, along with cold compresses, which eased his pain. Thankfully, Larry did not break any bones, but he did have a sprained neck and was very sore, especially in his back. In spite of Larry's accident, trails were hiked, mountains explored, and the Colorado Rocky Mountains viewed while riding the historic Durango-Silverton steam engine train.

When Larry and I were exploring God's creation, it felt as if time was standing still. The scenery, God's creative artwork, always changed as the wind blew or the sun set. Words cannot express the deep comfort we felt in these moments when we stood in awe at our surroundings. Larry longed to be in nature. He did not look forward to returning home to doctor's appointments.

Chapter 18 Colorado

*Larry and Tammy exploring God's creation at
Piedra River Trailhead in Colorado.*

Chapter 19

Surgery

Larry had a CAT scan on August 17, 2010. On Friday, August 20, Larry and I were sitting in the oncologist's exam room waiting for the results. As I was sitting and waiting, I felt as if I was in a boxing ring. Time had elapsed since Larry's diagnosis and I dreaded hearing more negative news. With each minute I waited, I felt as if I was being punched harder and harder. The doctor would soon walk through the door with the results. I was tense, anticipating his words, which I figured would knock the wind right out of me.

Dr. Ebert (pseudonym), Larry's oncologist, began comparing Larry's recent scan with his first scan. There was notably significant growth of the cancer cells in the liver. Dr. Ebert is a very frank speaker. He bluntly said, "Larry's cancer in the liver is aggressive. It has and will continue to enlarge exponentially from 2 to 4 millimeters, 4 to 8, 8 to 16, etc. The colon tumor, however, has remained the same."

Larry never discussed these results further with me. I once initiated the discussion, and Larry said he did not want to talk about it. He said if he did, he felt as if he was dying. "Instead, I want to focus on living," Larry said. Out of compassion and empathy for my husband, I never brought up test results again. He shared his feelings with me and

Chapter 19 Surgery

I respected them. In the future, Larry's doctors handed the results of lab work or CAT scans directly to me.

On September 1, 2010, Larry had a repeat colonoscopy since his abdominal pain was getting more obnoxious. This time the procedure was with a different surgeon who used a pediatric scope, hoping to slip past the colon blockage with the smaller size scope. But like the first, he could not get past the tumor. The recommendation was to admit Larry for surgery since he was already prepped. The oncologist and surgeon agreed it was just a matter of time before Larry would have total blockage and experience extreme pain.

The surgery lasted three hours, and the surgeon removed three feet of Larry's large intestine. He said Larry should not have any problems except that he would have to use the restroom more often. During surgery the surgeon was also able to get a biopsy of the liver.

Soon after Larry returned to his room, the nurses wanted him to walk a short distance, but Larry wanted to walk even farther. He always pushed himself! Often, he proudly stated he was a stubborn Swede, and he used his stubbornness to his advantage. He slowly walked the perimeter of his hospital wing three times, waving and smiling each time as he passed by the nurses' station. He had plans and he would do anything to speed his recovery.

Prior to Larry's surgery his oncologist signed life insurance papers predicting, in his opinion, a life span of less than ninety days. When Dr. Ebert handed the envelope to me, he said, "Remember, it is just a number." As devastating as this was, this signature gave us a $50,000 advance on his life insurance and enabled him to fulfill his dream of finding an affordable motor home. Traveling was therapeutic for Larry and doing so in a motor home would be so much easier for him. At any given time, the home on wheels could provide a comfortable place of rest. Why not pursue his retirement dream as long as he was able? After hours of searching the web, Larry found a motor home in Grand Rapids, Michigan, that caught his attention.

Chapter 20

The "Dutchess"

On Wednesday, September 15, 2010, Larry had his staples removed, and remarkably on Thursday we were in Michigan attending training at an RV dealership. The pictures of the motor home Larry found on the Internet led us to a private seller in Grand Rapids. However, after touring the motor home, we realized the pictures had been deceiving. Larry was disappointed to hit a dead end, but suggested visiting an RV dealership in the area before returning home. At Midway RV Center, Larry and I toured a meticulously clean, diesel motor home with only 70,000 miles on it. I especially loved the hardwood floors and large kitchen space. The purchase price was $58,000, which Larry and I paid in full that afternoon. After a brief training session, we drove the motor home off the lot and stopped at his niece's home in Niles, Michigan for the remaining weekend. Five months had passed since we had spent the weekend with this family right before his diagnosis in April.

At a follow-up appointment, Larry's surgeon confirmed cancer in the liver from the biopsy he had performed. During surgery Larry had 104 lymph nodes removed from his abdomen. The pathology report showed that out of the 104 lymph nodes removed, remarkably, only one had cancer. His surgeon said that out of all his years of doing surgery, he had

Chapter 20 The "Dutchess"

never come across a situation like that before. Cancer would not hold Larry back. He was ready to fulfill some lifelong dreams. He had joy in his heart and a new bounce in his step. I respected and admired his faith and attitude. For us, living with cancer meant planning, exploring, and living life. Larry and I embraced challenges and opportunities.

> *For us, living with cancer meant planning, exploring, and living life. Larry and I embraced challenges and opportunities.*

    As the first road trip neared, Larry knew he had to find a new home for Buddy. I am allergic to pet dander and had to use an inhaler when I was in an enclosed space with the dog. It was hard to breathe when Buddy and I were in the same house, so it would certainly not work at all for us to both be in the motor home together. Larry and I also felt uncomfortable leaving him in the motor home for long periods while we went exploring. Larry's friend, Kevin, from Hustedt Jewelers once told Larry he would love to have an obedient dog like Buddy. Remembering this, Larry contacted him to see if he would be interested in adopting Buddy, and he was. This was a difficult transition for Larry, but passing Buddy to a friend made it easier for him. Buddy went to work with Kevin at the jewelry store every day. He was a sociable dog and greeted customers in the store. Later we heard that customers would drop by the store just to see Buddy. Larry looked forward to visiting him in between road trips.

    The motor home was a Newmar Dutch Star, and Larry decided to name her "Dutchess." Where would the Dutchess go on her first road trip? Larry suggested the Northwest and I agreed. A few days would be spent in South Dakota while en route to Yellowstone National Park. On the trip home, Larry and I would tour the state of Utah. National parks were of special interest to both of us. While reviewing a map, Larry and I noticed many national parks in Utah.

*Larry driving the Dutch Star, Camry in tow,
through the Badlands in South Dakota.*

In South Dakota, we stayed at a motor home park with a view of the Badlands. Close by was a hiking trail. Since Larry was recovering from surgery, he didn't walk far, but I continued on up the trail and took a picture of him from high above.

Posing for a picture in the Badlands.

Chapter 20 The "Dutchess" 65

Hiking in the Badlands.

Another adventure in South Dakota was driving through a park called Bear Country. Instructions were given to keep windows and doors closed at all times. The car was the cage, while the bears, buffalo, and coyotes roamed freely. This was fun and exhilarating. Like others before me and after me, I risked rolling down the window long enough to take a few great pictures.

Bears taking a leisurely stroll at Bear Country USA drive-through wildlife park.

At the end of the drive, Larry and I enjoyed watching two bear cubs play. The small cubs were getting very frisky while balancing on a tree limb, and it was obvious one of them would lose the battle and fall. My video camera was rolling, and I was ready to capture the entire event on film. The final push came, and I heard spectators gasp, expecting the cub to fall. Instead, his paws grasped the limb, and he swung like an acrobat in the circus. Larry smiled, and I smiled. Larry laughed, and I laughed.

Chapter 21

Wyoming

Larry and I enjoyed a short visit to Mount Rushmore before arriving in Cody, Wyoming. The scenery and wildlife in Wyoming was spectacular. The campground, reserved for one week, had mountains surrounding its perimeter. The best thing of all was that it was only twenty miles from Yellowstone National Park. By now, we had a routine down for hooking up the utilities, and unhooking the car. We were proud to have the Dutchess set up within half an hour upon arriving at the campsite.

Crossing the state line into Wyoming.

The next morning, at the crack of dawn, we were sitting in the car at the east entrance of Yellowstone. Immediately after entering the park, Larry noticed a beautiful lake on the left that beckoned us to come closer to admire its beauty. The reflection of the trees on the lake projected an image even more beautiful than the trees themselves. I will never forget what Larry said while standing and gazing at this lake. Larry has been an avid reader his entire life. While facing the calm, tranquil lake, hands in his pockets, he said, "I have been reading about this place, and I have wanted to see it ever since I was nine years old." Larry was fifty-eight years old and grateful for the opportunity to experience the awe-inspiring beauty Yellowstone offered. Hearing him speak these words reiterated to me that this was exactly where we needed to be. Together, Larry and I thanked the Lord for this opportunity.

Letting off some steam at Yellowstone National Park.

It only takes two words, magnificent and majestic, to describe Yellowstone National Park and Grand Teton National Park. Larry and I heard steam vents hiss, mud pots blurp, and geysers gush. The mountains, waterfalls, and wildlife were spectacular. This truly was the home where the buffalos roamed. Traffic jams were often created when the wild beasts decided to take over the road. These adjacent parks are a videographer or photographer's haven. One of my favorite pictures is the golden orange aspen trees lined gracefully in front of the lake and mountain at Grand Teton National Park.

Mirrored mountains at Grand Teton National Park.

Golden orange aspen trees at Grand Teton National Park.

At Yellowstone Larry and I were blessed to watch Old Faithful give her stunning performance twice in one day. The first eruption began shortly after we arrived. We noticed people gathering so we rushed to find a suitable viewing spot. It was time for lunch, so after dining at the Old Faithful Inn, ninety minutes had elapsed and the timing was just right to watch her graceful act a second time.

Larry and I decided to enjoy more of the Northwest by taking a three-hour drive on Bear Tooth Pass, America's most scenic highway. The drive into the state of Montana was impressive with mountains, lakes, and curvy roads. Normally, Wyoming and Montana have cool weather in September (sometimes even snow), but it was exceptionally warm, in the 70s and 80s all week.

Larry and I attended The Cody Seventh-day Adventist Church in Wyoming for two weeks and acquired some new friends. These new acquaintances blessed us with the gift of hospitality. Invitations were extended for lunch in their homes or to social events. One Sabbath afternoon we were invited to join a group hike. Larry was tired and wanted to rest, but he encouraged me to go. With hesitation, I joined the group. After getting out of the car, I took a picture of a sign that said, "WARNING, BEAR TERRITORY."

I asked the leader of the group if this area was safe, and he said, "Yes. I hike here with a group of people every weekend." He put my nerves at ease, just a little, by telling me there is safety in numbers. He said a bear would not bother people in a group, but it would, however, target an individual. I enjoyed the hike, while constantly thinking, "What if we come across more than one bear?"

Larry was able to share his testimony in Cody. I was proud of him and pleased. When he spoke, everyone listened. We did not know the impact this conversation had. The seeds of faith and trust were planted and the cultivation would occur through the Lord.

On the morning of October 3, 2010, Larry and I broke camp in Wyoming and hit the road again. Larry was experiencing abdominal pain off and on, and it concerned me more than it concerned him. Larry did not complain. He rarely said anything about how he felt, so when I heard him voice any complaints, they were concerning to me. I wondered if he should continue driving or return home? *How long, Lord? How much time do I have with Larry? How do I prepare for the inevitable?* When these questions erupted in my mind, I gave them right back to the Lord. He is the only one who knows the beginning and the end. He had been faithful in the past, and I knew He would be faithful in the future.

Chapter 21 Wyoming

How long, Lord?
How much time do I have with Larry?
How do I prepare for the inevitable?

The panoramic view while driving in the motor home was an experience itself. Often, we would cross a bridge or make a turn and eagerly gaze out the window at the unexpected beauty. Larry knew I loved the Carpenters as a child, so he purchased a double CD for me before we began traveling. The words to the song "We've Only Just Begun" became lyrics with a personal, special meaning. Larry and I were living these words.

Chapter 22

Utah

When crossing a long bridge into Utah, we both let out a simultaneous sigh. At times, words could not describe the beauty, so sighs seemed most appropriate. Larry then said, "Wow! Look at that!" Larry spoke reassuring, short words of affirmation. It was therapeutic for us to be sharing horizons.

The country drive through the small towns of Utah was peaceful. Each town announced a friendly welcome with streets adorned with cascading flowers in hanging baskets, cozy shops, one-of-a-kind restaurants, and potted plants meticulously placed on sidewalks.

Larry and I chose to settle for a few days in the small town of Leeds. The motor home park was close to Zion National Park. We set up camp quickly and retired early. Unfortunately, the night rain kept me awake. Even though it was a long, dreamless night, the rain soothed my soul. I reflected on the analogy between sun and joy and rain and pain. The storms in my life help me to appreciate all that is good. The rain did not let up in the morning. Larry and I toured Zion National Park in the rain. We could not cross trails at times due to flooding. Campgrounds had been reserved in advance, so the next day it was time to move on. Before leaving town, I purchased a sticker in a local store that said,

Chapter 22 Utah

"Home is where my motor home takes me." The Dutchess was our home away from home.

Our next stop was Moab, Utah, where it was 74 degrees and sunny. The red rock was stunning, and everything seemed to be named after red rock. Larry and I noticed the Red Rock Mall, Red Rock Restaurant, and Red Rock stores, in which you could purchase Red Rock t-shirts.

We parked the Dutchess at Archview RV Park, close to Canyonland National Park and Arches National Park. At this country RV park in Utah, Larry and I met Jim and Debb Rhyce. Jim and Debb had four bulldogs traveling with them. Since Larry is a dog lover, it didn't take long for these dogs, and their owners, to catch his attention. While Jim and Debb were walking their dogs, struggling to keep leashes from tangling, Larry struck up a conversation with them. Larry had previously asked me to never bring up the subject of his cancer whenever he or I crossed paths with new acquaintances. Larry did not want any pity. He said he felt as if people looked at and treated him differently when they found out about his diagnosis. However, the situation was different with Jim and Debb. Larry shared his cancer journey with this warm, caring couple from Louisiana. When we parted, the Rhyce family continued to stay in touch, following Larry's journey on Caring Bridge.

The Delicate Arch at Arches National Park in Utah.

The rock formations at Arches National Park were extraordinary. Larry and I liked everything about Utah. Larry mentioned that it would be a nice place to live, and I agreed.

Enjoying rock formations at Arches National Park.

All this exploring and all these adventures were healthy for Larry's soul, and mine. While leaving Arches National Park, Larry stopped the car and asked for the camera. Usually, I was the photographer so this caught me by surprise. Larry rolled down the window and snapped a picture of some intriguing cloud formations in odd shapes with strokes of intermingled sunlight. We both reveled in the beauty of God's creation.

Larry's snapshot of God's artwork.

Chapter 23

A Week at Home

  While on the road, we sometimes stayed overnight at a rest stop or perhaps in a Walmart parking lot. A rest stop in Iowa allowed us a good place to rest and served as a final stop before returning to Paxton, Illinois. On October 13, 2010, we walked through our back door and were stunned at the unbelievable amount of mail that Margaret had again graciously collected. The junk mail was quickly sorted and tossed, leaving bills, insurance, and disability papers that required immediate attention. Blessings were found in the abundance of encouraging cards sent by family and friends. These messages of inspiration were priceless.

  In a card that said, "Amazing things can happen …," my friend and former employer said, "Both of you have been amazing to watch as you have faced this cancer together. Your trust in God and support of one another is a witness to so many! Our family will continue to pray for your healing, Larry, and for the adventure you are heading out on."

  Larry received many cards from former customers. One in particular that Larry treasured was from Gary and Debra McCullough, owners and general manager of WGCY radio station in Gibson City in which they wrote, "Larry, Gary and I were saddened to hear of your illness. Our thoughts and prayers are with you and your wife. We will always have fond memories of your days as our friendly FedEx deliveryman. We hope you can take comfort from friends and family at this time."

I was touched when I received a card addressed specifically to me. Wendy wrote, "Dear Tammy, I just wanted to let you know that not only is Larry in my prayers but you also. Thank you for taking good care of my dear friend. I don't know what it's been like for you, not having been in your shoes, but I'm sure the Lord is leading somehow to not only strengthen your faith but others too."

Larry and I even received messages from people we did not know. In a card from the Illinois Seventh-day Adventist Conference, Pastor Stan Hagen said, "Dear Brother Smestad, May God's blessing be with you as you stand in need. We are praying for you." To know friends, family, and fellow Christians were praying was uplifting.

Larry was still doing much better than his doctors had expected. However, the words previously spoken by the doctor, "things can change fast," stuck in my mind. At Larry's recent appointment, Dr. Ebert said, "Keep doing what you're doing. It seems to be working for you." Regardless of Larry's lifestyle changes, he felt the reason he was doing well was because of prayers. Larry asked me to post on Caring Bridge how thankful he was for all the prayers!

On October 18, 2010, Larry had a blood test, which again showed several markers elevated. His potassium was dangerously high. Due to the results, he was instructed to return immediately for an EKG. The results of the EKG were good, but he was advised to not eat foods high in potassium and to stop further use of herbal remedies. Also, there was a drastic leap in his CEA test. The numbers jumped from 9.8 to 21.2. Dr. Ebert simply said, "His liver function is deteriorating."

Larry and I had the next road trip planned, and he was still determined to go.

Chapter 24

Nashville and the Gulf Shores

With the motor home loaded, we left Paxton on October 20, 2010. The itinerary for this trip included four days in Nashville, a couple of days in Chattanooga and a week in Gulf Shores, Alabama. Tyler and I both share October birthdays, so Tyler and his girlfriend, Amelia, provided tickets to celebrate at the Grand Ole Opry on the evening of my birthday. The facility offered a group tour during the day, so the four of us attended a backstage tour prior to the evening performance. It was interesting to see the dressing rooms and exhilarating to stand on the stage where dreams had been fulfilled for many country stars.

I treasure the picture an employee took of Larry and me wearing cowboy hats while holding a guitar and ukulele. Tyler and Amelia have an identical picture as well. Larry loved country music, just like both of my sons. At the Opry, he was in his element. It was a memorable moment for Blake Shelton as well, since he was inducted into the Country Hall of Fame that evening. While this was entertaining and enjoyable for me, the highlight was time spent with family.

Chapter 24 Nashville and the Gulf Shores

Larry and Tammy jammin' at the Grand Ole Opry.

Larry and I drove to Chattanooga because he had made arrangements to meet high school friends who lived in the area. During a few of Larry's high school years he attended Broadview Academy, a Seventh-day Adventist boarding school in Illinois. Larry was excited about reuniting with a few of these classmates. These friends had been following Larry's journey on Caring Bridge and looked forward to a reunion with him. While dining at a local Mediterranean restaurant, there was stimulating conversation, reminiscing, and laughter. The following day we visited the Tennessee Aquarium and toured the historic Chattanooga Choo-Choo.

Before leaving Nashville, Larry had unhooked the car from the Dutchess and left it with Tyler who then drove the car with Amelia to the motor home park in order to join us on the next road trip. We were so excited to have them along for the next adventure. Larry grinned ear to ear as he sat behind the wheel of the motor home early the following morning. I sat in the comfortable, reclining passenger seat, while Tyler and Amelia remained on the couch. "This is the way to travel," I said as Larry hit the horn just for fun.

On the road again...

On Wednesday, October 27, 2010, the Dutchess arrived at the reserved campsite in Alabama. After setting up camp, everyone anxiously jumped in the car, eager to view the beaches in Gulf Shores. On the short drive, Tyler and Amelia noticed a tie-dye store. Everything was tie-dye including the building, a van outside, and, of course, all clothing inside. Everyone picked out tie-dye t-shirts, and being the shutterbug I am, I proudly snapped a group picture. Larry proceeded to drive by the beach for a glance while the sun was setting.

Chapter 24 Nashville and the Gulf Shores

*Larry and Tammy with Tyler and Amelia at
B&L's Happy Shak Boutique in Gulf Shores.*

    Larry and I joined several motor home clubs in order to receive discounts at campsites. This particular motor home park in Gulf Shores was listed in the catalog. After walking through the office door, my initial impression was that it looked more like a shack than a building. Attached to the so-called office building was a fence where a potbelly pig lived. Was this a mascot, or was this pig their pet? I do not find anything attractive about potbelly pigs, and this poor pig had a large wart on his snout, which did not add to his beauty whatsoever. *Well, we are in the Deep South*, I thought. After looking at the pool, which was not well maintained, Larry and I apologized to Tyler and Amelia. Unlike every other park we had previously stayed at, this one, in particular, would not be one to recommend. Despite the potbelly pig and the pool, the campsite where the motor home was parked was absolutely beautiful, adorned with tall pine trees.

The Dutchess taking a break in Gulf Shores.

    Larry, Tyler, Amelia, and I arrived early in the morning at the Gulf Shores beach. Larry and I sat together in blue and white striped beach chairs under an umbrella while attentively watching Tyler and Amelia. After years of studying hard at college, the two of them were experiencing a long overdue vacation. I could see how soothing and rejuvenating this was to both of them, as it was to us. As soon as their feet touched the sand and eyes caught the waves, something happened. Hand in hand they ran, jumped, and splashed in the water. My favorite pictures in Gulf Shores were taken at sunset. These pictures are a great example of what cancer cannot do. Cancer has no control over joy and love.

Chapter 24 Nashville and the Gulf Shores

Tyler and Amelia's joyful leap.

Larry and Tammy's sunset stroll.

Lambert's Café (known for "throwed rolls") was located close to the motor home park. The restaurant was highly recommended, so Larry and I decided to treat Tyler and Amelia for dinner. The restaurant décor was interesting. It included antiques, canning jars for glasses, old wooden floors, and employees wearing blue jeans and plaid dress shirts. Additionally, the men wore suspenders and bow ties. After ordering a main entrée, waiters and waitresses meandered around tables with large kettle pots, enticing you to try whatever was inside. It was a rather noisy atmosphere as the waiters, or waitresses, hollered "Grits, grits, anyone want to try some grits?" or "I've got macaroni and tomatoes. Macaroni and tomatoes, anyone?" How could you not smile and enjoy this dining experience? Appetizers were sampled by all, leaving everyone full before the main entrée even arrived. Next, a man came through pushing a cart full of warm rolls. The scent of freshly baked bread permeated the room. Unexpectedly, people began raising their hands in the air and the man started tossing rolls throughout the entire restaurant. Of course, we all joined in the fun. This was much more than a restaurant. It was a dining experience, and everyone wanted to return a second time. The second time around I brought my camera.

Dining at Lambert's Café, home of the "throwed rolls."

The four of us all love white, sandy beaches, so since Pensacola, Florida, is a short distance from Gulf Shores, we all agreed to spend the next day there. It was a beautiful change in scenery. The beach had soft, white sand. October was the perfect time to visit because we had the beach almost all to ourselves.

Chapter 24 Nashville and the Gulf Shores

Larry and Tammy enjoying the white, sandy beach at Pensacola.

Larry searching for seashells by the seashore.

Tyler and Amelia joined Larry in his search for seashells. I sat and watched them while taking pictures and storing the memories in my heart. Barbara Streisand's song "The Way We Were" came to my mind. I recalled the lyrics about memories remaining and reminding us of "the way we were."

I am very thankful God does not reveal the future. If He did, would I have married Larry, knowing I would lose him so soon? I felt humbled and blessed that God had chosen me to walk beside Larry. I was hand-picked by God to be right where I was at this specific moment in time. I thanked Jesus for the opportunity to be Larry's wife. I asked Him to carry me faithfully through this journey when I would no longer have the strength to walk, to stand, or to speak.

Larry, Tyler, and Amelia soon approached me with seashells and smiles. I quickly dried my tears and put on a happy face. Everyone was hungry, so it was time to enjoy the picnic lunch I had prepared. Cranes gracefully strolled nearby, while seagulls happily ate leftovers. Words cannot express how therapeutic this was. Cancer, the uninvited guest, was there as usual, lurking in the shadows. But joy cast out sorrow.

Words cannot express how therapeutic this was.

A crane making footprints in the sand.

Chapter 24 Nashville and the Gulf Shores

After four days of enjoying beaches and fine dining, between Pensacola and Gulf Shores, the week came to an end. Larry and I drove Tyler and Amelia back to Nashville before returning to Illinois. Larry decided to visit his brother, Brad, and sister-in-law, Deb, in Indiana on the way home. Larry and I arrived in Paxton on Sunday, November 7, 2010.

Chapter 25

FedEx Cares

Since Larry and I were spending more time on the road than home, Paxton didn't seem like home anymore. Larry's parents lived just thirty minutes away and my entire family, except for Tyler, lived an hour away. Home meant time with family (including church family) and friends. The downside of being back "home" was dealing with the reality of cancer.

As usual, after returning home, Larry had many appointments. Larry's recent lab work showed an increase in the CEA from 21.2 to 24.3. His potassium, which had been high last month, was now in the normal range. Just when something got into the normal range, something else became abnormal. Now Larry's phosphate was high. It tested at 182, and the normal range is around 121. Larry was scheduled for a repeat CAT scan in two weeks. The scans are what I dreaded the most. On the CAT scan, I could see the enemy. Cancer was seeking to destroy my husband's liver. I hated cancer like God hates sin.

Previously, while on the road, one of Larry's coworkers had called him. He informed Larry that FedEx was planning a benefit to honor him and raise funds to help with expenses. November 20, 2010, was the proposed date. Larry had a very close relationship with his customers and colleagues. He had been well respected in the community, and he had

Chapter 25 FedEx Cares 89

regretted not having the opportunity to say goodbye. After Larry's colonoscopy in April, he had not returned to work, so he hadn't said goodbye to anyone. Larry was appreciative and thankful for an opportunity to reconnect with his FedEx coworkers and customers.

FedEx poster advertising Larry's benefit.

From the perspective of FedEx and Larry's customers, this was a way to show appreciation and respect to Larry. And that is exactly what they did. It was a very emotional event for us. FedEx employees wore t-shirts that said, "FedEx Cares," with Larry's badge number (30025) on the t-shirt. I choked up when I walked in the door and saw the t-shirts, and Larry choked up when Buddy walked in the door with his new owner, Kevin.

Larry was never fond of having to wear a uniform to work every day. So it was quite humorous when the staff presented him with a quilt sewn from used uniforms. This became a treasured item! Many local merchants donated merchandise and services for the silent auction. Volunteers busily worked the food service line. Larry and I were extremely touched by this event.

Larry boldly walked up front and grabbed the microphone from the master of ceremony. In a noisy room, there was now complete silence. Larry held back tears while he said, "Yes, my wife and I are having the time of our life traveling, but I want you to know," Larry paused while looking down, "I miss you guys. Thank you."

Two weeks later, FedEx presented Larry and I with a $5,400 check to help with expenses.

Chapter 26

Bucket List

On November 29, 2010, Larry had another CAT scan. Within a couple of days, Larry and I discussed the ominous results with the oncologist. Dr. Ebert said, "The cancer is starting to get more aggressive. In comparing this scan with the scan from just three months ago, there has been significant growth." Out of respect to Larry, he handed the results to me. Larry heard Dr. Ebert's words. He was not in denial. However, when he left the exam room, as was his custom, Larry left what was said behind.

Larry had the terminal illness, but I felt a part of myself slowly dying as well. Visually, I could see changes in Larry. The weight loss was very noticeable in his face and arms, while his abdomen and legs were swollen. At times he itched, which I read was a sign of liver failure. *How long, Lord? How do I prepare?* What a heart wrenching process this was to watch and witness on a daily basis.

Larry was already planning the next trip. During an evening at home, we had written a "bucket list" of seventeen items. The list included places to visit and fun things to do. If everything on the list were accomplished, Larry and I would create a second list. The first list included:

- Buying a motor home
- Visiting Yellowstone National Park
- Visiting Arches National Park
- Swimming with dolphins
- Parasailing
- Visiting Sanibel Island
- Going scuba diving
- Taking a Hawaiian cruise
- Riding on a zip line
- Seeing the New England states
- Visiting Niagara Falls
- Buying a Corvette convertible
- Visiting Alaska again
- Taking a road trip on Route 66 in the Corvette
- Riding in a hot air balloon
- Visiting Yosemite National Park
- Visiting Sequoia National Park.

The bucket list was sitting nearby on the coffee table. Larry glanced at it and commented, "Several things on the list have already been accomplished. I am going to cross them off." As quickly as he grabbed the pen, I yelled, "Wait." I grabbed my video camera and captured Larry's hand crossing accomplished items off the list. In the future I had plans to incorporate this video clip into a home movie called "Our Bucket List."

Chapter 27

Testimony

  Larry and I thanked and praised God every day for His unfathomable love and goodness. God could not be wearied or overburdened even though we were. God graciously gave us strength sufficient for each day. Through God's grace, Larry shared his testimony whenever and wherever God opened doors. This often occurred informally in churches we visited and in homes where we were welcomed guests. Larry was always open and willing to share God's goodness and faithfulness.
  Like many cancer patients, Larry felt partly responsible for his illness. He wanted to impress upon others the importance of taking care of their bodies. During Larry's single years, he did not make healthy choices. While lifestyle and diet play a major role in a person's health, I did not want Larry to beat himself up over the matter. In December we were given the opportunity to speak formally for the first time at the All Nations Seventh-day Adventist Church in Bloomington, Illinois.
  Together, Larry and I worked on a PowerPoint presentation that included scriptures and pictures to illustrate our message. Larry began the presentation by sharing his diagnosis and encouraging everyone to be more "in-tune" with his or her body. Larry always had a passion for automobiles so he related the human body to a car. "When properly maintained,

the car, or human body, will run well," Larry said. "You wouldn't think of putting anything but fuel in your gas tank. You could damage your car irreparably if you put something other than fuel in it. The same goes for our bodies." He continued, "Your car comes with an owner's manual. For most of us, it is unread and stored in the glove compartment. Our bodies, intricately designed in the image of our Creator, also come with an owner's manual. It is the Bible."

I closed the presentation by briefly discussing the eight laws of health, often presented at Adventist health seminars. The eight laws of health are addressed by using the acronym "NEWSTART"—"N" stands for nutrition, "E" for exercise, "W" for water, "S" for sunlight, "T" for temperance, "A" for air, "R" for rest, and "T" for trust in God. From God's Word, I read, "So whether you eat or drink or whatever you do, do it all for the glory of God" (1 Cor. 10:31).

Chapter 28

Christmas

Larry looked forward to December 2010 for many reasons. First of all, he would no longer be working overtime, overwhelmed with deliveries, as he had been for many years around the holidays. Because of this, Larry said he would enjoy Christmas this year more than ever. Secondly, Larry had planned the next road trip, a warm winter in Florida. But most importantly, Christmas was a time to show gratitude to God.

Larry and I reveled in time spent with family and friends during the holidays. Attending Christmas programs, listening to Christmas carols, and singing the hymns in church filled our hearts with the joy of the season. Additionally, I was able to attend a Gaither concert with my friend, Rhonda, which was a spiritual blessing.

Larry and I also enjoyed shopping together. Larry felt impressed to give small gifts to people he ordinarily did not buy for. When he gave these small gifts to family and friends, it was as if he was saying, "You are important to me. I am a better person today because you have been a part of my life. Through this gift, I want you to remember how thankful I am for you. I want you to always know how much I love you."

Larry and I enjoyed a Christmas Eve celebration in our home with Travis and Heather and Tyler and Amelia. After prayer and a shared dinner, we gathered in the family room to exchange and open gifts. This would most likely be Larry's last Christmas. That was a known fact though it did not spoil the celebration. There was love and laughter. The ability to love one another, to renew our faith, and to bring hope into our lives and the lives of others is what Christmas means to me. Faith, hope, and love are character traits to always hold near and dear to our hearts, especially during Christmas when we reflect on the miraculous birth of Jesus.

On Christmas day, Larry and I had dinner at his parents' home. No one expected the emotional exchange that occurred after dinner. Larry turned to his niece, Laura and said, "Do you remember when you were around nine years old you told me you wanted my ruby ring someday. I haven't forgotten your request." Laura responded with a stunned look on her face. She nodded as she recalled the conversation she had as a little girl with her Uncle Larry. Knowing that Larry brought this to her attention because he was dying struck an emotional chord with her and everyone in the room. Larry intended to honor the request of his niece.

No one expected the emotional exchange that occurred after dinner.

I had never seen this ring before. I knew by description it was red, and I knew Laura admired it, but Larry hadn't been able to remember where it was. Often, between trips, Larry searched for the ring. Sometimes I would forget about the search and ask him what he was looking for. He would say, "I'm looking for the ring. I have to find that ring."

During the holiday season, I experienced a noticeable change in my thinking. Larry was much worse since his diagnosis in April. The initial shock had worn off and reality had set in. My thought process shifted from, *How long, Lord?* to *How do I say goodbye?* My emotions were all over the place. I had strength, but fear. I had joy, but sorrow.

Many people partnered in prayer with me for Larry. Apparently, God did not intend to heal Larry, but His continued presence gave us peace and hope. Having friends and family walk beside us during this difficult journey was a comfort. Larry's uncomplaining, courageous attitude additionally gave me strength. When he prayed, he asked for God's will to be done. He often said, "Your will, God, is the one that matters."

I admit, watching Larry's body deteriorate was horrific. I made the choice to look at Larry as if he was not sick. I focused on Larry's eyes and his smile and maintained a mental picture of the strong healthy man I had fallen in love with. One particular morning while Larry was looking

Chapter 28 Christmas

at himself in the mirror, turning from side to side, he disgustingly said, "I don't want to look at myself anymore. I look like a P.O.W."

I responded, "I don't think so."

He said, "OK, then, I look like a starving Ethiopian."

I said, "That's not what I see. I see my strong, handsome Larry."

He had the last word by saying, "I sure am glad you have a good imagination."

Even though Larry's lab tests continued to show decline in his liver function, he reassured me he felt well enough for the next road trip. I had reservations. Many "what ifs" were going through my mind. What if Larry took a turn for the worse while far away from home? He would not want to die in Florida. What if Larry was not able to drive the motor home any longer? I was comfortable driving on the interstate but not through city streets. I did not trust myself in making sharp turns, especially while towing the car. I appreciated friends or family members volunteering to help, if need be. Ellen's husband, Rick, was one of those volunteers and my brother-in-law, Brad, was another. Both of them offered to fly to Florida and drive the motor home back to Illinois if Larry was in distress. Having contingency plans in place for some of the unknowns provided a degree of comfort.

The next trip would be a long one. It included two months in Florida, a drive to Arlington, Texas, followed by a seven-day Hawaiian cruise with his sister, Ann, and her husband, Don. I wondered if this would be too much for Larry. I recalled what the doctor said, "Maybe you'll have one year." I quickly dismissed that thought. The holidays were over and the winter months in Illinois were not pleasant. It would be refreshing for Larry to be in sunshine, getting exercise, and experiencing new things. Besides, there were many items on the bucket list to be accomplished in Florida and Hawaii.

Chapter 29

The Sunshine State

On January 2, 2011, Larry and I parked the Dutchess in Valdosta, Georgia, at a campground called Eagle's Roost. It was a beautiful lot with Spanish moss draping off every tree. The Dutchess was in the swamps!

Motor home park in Valdosta, Georgia.

Chapter 29 The Sunshine State

The following day Larry and I visited St. Simons Island and Jekyll Island. Larry and I enjoyed the beauty of Georgia before moving on to Florida. Understandably, motor home parks fill up quickly in Florida during the winter months. When I called to make arrangements, I learned other travelers had made reservations a year in advance. Knowing this, it was an answer to prayer to find availability anywhere. Our Florida itinerary included three days at Disney World, a month at Kissimmee, and two weeks at the KOA in St. Petersburg.

Kissimmee, Florida, was a great place to settle for a month. Larry and I were very pleased to be out of the city at a campground in the country that was near a large lake. Having horses on the acreage right beside the campground was an unexpected bonus. A sign was posted on the fence that said "Police Training Site." Larry and I enjoyed watching the horses train on obstacle courses in preparation for service on the police force. The lake and horses made this campground a peaceful place to take long walks. Additionally, Larry and I took advantage of the local airboat ride the campground offered.

Airboat ride at Eastlake Fish Camp in Kissimmee, Florida.

When Larry and I drove into the city to buy groceries, I purchased a map of lighthouses in Florida, which led to another fun scavenger hunt. The first lighthouse we visited was located on the Ponce de Leon Inlet in Central Florida. The dark red lighthouse is the tallest in the state of Florida and one of the tallest lighthouses in the United States. Larry patiently waited while I climbed 175 feet (203 steps) to the top. From there I enjoyed a breathtaking view of the Florida coastline. After leaving Ponce de Leon, we drove to St. Augustine to tour and take pictures of the beautiful black and white striped lighthouse built there in 1874.

Tammy at Ponce de Leon lighthouse.

With Kissimmee being so close to Orlando, during the month of January, Larry and I were able to experience many Orlando attractions. At least twice a week, Larry and I left the campground for a "fun day." Sea World, Universal Studios, Ripley's Believe It or Not, Gatorland, and several beaches kept Larry active and engaged.

Larry at John's Pass.

Chapter 29 The Sunshine State

Larry in oversized chair at Ripley's Believe It or Not!

One evening while we were driving in Kissimmee looking for a Mexican restaurant, Larry noticed an advertisement for the Mecum Automobile Auction. Since Larry had a special interest in automobiles, especially collector cars, attending the Mecum Automobile Auction was added on the "fun things to do and see" list. Larry had always been a car fan. NASCAR was a passion of his, and he followed his favorite driver, Denny Hamlin, whose sponsor was FedEx.

During another "fun" afternoon, while driving around near Orlando, we came across Roger's Corvette Center in Maitland, Florida. This was a dealership that sold only Corvettes with classic models from the many years the Chevrolet Corvette had been manufactured. The sight of the specialty car lot immediately grabbed Larry's interest. "Do you mind if we stop and look around?" he asked. I agreed. After all, it would be fascinating to see this beautiful car in its many variations over the years.

To Larry's great surprise, many of the models had fairly low mileage, as their previous owners had primarily used them as their prized toys and not their primary mode of transportation. The prices were quite reasonable, especially given the pristine appearances of these collectors' autos. Larry found a pewter 2001 Corvette convertible with only a little over 10,000 miles on it, and it was love at first sight. He weighed the pros and cons of this special purchase with me. It would fulfill a lifelong dream. Neither Larry nor I knew how much more time God would give him, and neither Larry nor I had planned to buy a car when he pulled into Roger's

Corvette Center, but we decided to go for it. Before we drove off the lot in our 2000 Toyota Camry, we had placed a down payment deposit on this beautiful car. Another item was crossed off the bucket list.

On January 21, 2011, I posted this entry on the Caring Bridge website:

> Greetings to all our friends and family from the Sunshine State. Larry and I have had a wonderful week. After a few days of having a cold front (in the 60s), this week has been beautiful. It has been in the mid 70s all week. Larry and I started the week touring two lighthouses. One was in Ponce de Leon Inlet and the other at St. Augustine. They were both beautiful, and we took a lot of pictures.
>
> On Wednesday we went to Sea World. We really enjoyed all the shows there. Our campground hosts airboat rides, so we did this on Thursday. We didn't see any grown alligators, but we did see baby gators and many beautiful birds. Thursday evening Larry and I met with old friends of his from the Champaign Church who now live in Orlando. We enjoyed dinner together and had a wonderful visit. We are very grateful they are planning to come to the Kissimmee Church next week when we give our testimony.
>
> Larry is feeling rather well, and he is getting a lot of exercise. We appreciate your prayers, and we look forward to seeing you all soon!
>
> God Bless, Larry and Tammy!

On a Sabbath morning at the Kissimmee SDA Church, a woman seated directly behind me tapped me on the shoulder and asked, "Do I know you?" Before she got my attention, I had heard her speak. I whispered to Larry that I recognized her voice but could not remember how I knew her. She and I compared notes. Suddenly, she excitedly said, "I know! You are Tyler's mom." Janet Khan had been Tyler's kindergarten teacher at the Christian school he attended, and many years had passed since I had seen her. I recalled how beautifully she sang, sometimes in Spanish. I informed Janet that Larry and I would be sharing his story the following weekend. I eagerly asked her if she would open the presentation with special music.

On January 29, 2011, Janet sang one of my favorite songs, "His Eye is on the Sparrow." Larry then shared his testimony. He spoke of his diagnosis and how the Lord has strengthened, encouraged, and opened doors for him. Larry again stressed the importance of being aware of what your body is telling you. He repeated his comparison of the human body to a car. I spoke on the topic of nutrition, sharing the story of Daniel's decision to honor God with his diet when taken captive to Babylon. Together, Larry and I shared a message of faith and trust in God.

Larry sharing his testimony in Florida.

When we finished speaking, Wayne and Darlena Vogele, Larry's friends who live in Orlando, walked up front. In their hands was a quilt they presented to Larry. The "prayer quilt" was a gift of love made by a ministry team at the Forest Lake Seventh-day Adventist Church. In the middle of each panel, the ladies left a long string, encouraging others to tie a knot as they offered a special prayer for Larry. We were very thankful for this unexpected blessing!

The following Tuesday Larry addressed all the ladies in the prayer quilt ministry in Apopka, Florida. He shared his story and answered questions. On Wednesday morning Larry received a phone call from Pastor Sabine, one of the pastors at the Forest Lake Church. Larry accepted an invitation to attend prayer meeting on Wednesday evening.

This was the most spiritual prayer meeting Larry or I had ever attended. Pastor Sabine asked us to come forward as she spoke. She asked, "What would you like others to specifically pray about?" Larry answered by sharing his desire to be a witness throughout this journey. Larry and I both asked for prayers of faithfulness. During the prayer ceremony, Pastor Sabine anointed both of us. She later told me that she had planned on only anointing Larry but felt impressed to anoint me as well. Everyone prayed while laying hands on us. Needless to say, we left central Florida feeling very blessed!

On February 7, 2011, Larry and I moved a little farther south to St. Petersburg. After hooking up the motor home on the reserved lot at the St. Petersburg/Madeira Beach KOA, we took a short drive to explore the local surroundings. I had chosen this campground because it was the only one at which I could find availability, but I was pleasantly surprised to realize it was located just minutes away from the Gulf of Mexico's sandy beaches. John's Pass was nearby and was an enjoyable location from which we could walk the waterfront. Bubba Gump Shrimp Co. was a favorite locale for lunch whenever we visited John's Pass.

The St. Petersburg Pier, a landmark extending into Tampa Bay from downtown St. Petersburg, was another location we enjoyed. While at the pier, Larry and I paid $5.00 each to receive five fish with which to feed the pelicans on the boardwalk. "Stop and smell the roses" may be a cliché, but Larry and I enjoyed life's simple pleasures, which meant stopping to feed the pelicans on the pier.

Within a few days after arriving in St. Petersburg, Larry and I left the motor home and drove to the Florida Keys. He and I stayed three nights at The Paradise Inn, a bed and breakfast on Simonton Street in Key West, Florida. While on the road, I had searched websites looking for a suitable location to swim with dolphins. I had come across a site called Dolphins Plus in Key Largo, Florida. Swimming with dolphins can be rather expensive, but much to my surprise this company offered a program called, "Oma's Dolphin Swim." Oma was a cancer patient for six years. After she lost her battle to cancer, her family at Dolphins Plus, decided to honor her memory by offering complimentary dolphin swims to other cancer patients. Larry and I gratefully enrolled in both the structured dolphin swim and the natural dolphin swim.

Chapter 29 The Sunshine State

Love at first sight.

At Dolphins Plus in Key Largo, Florida.

During the structured swim, we were up close and personal with the dolphins. Larry especially loved touching and petting them. My favorite encounter was a push and pull activity. I started by holding my legs straight, on top of the water, with feet flexed. While in this position a dolphin quickly bumped my feet, pushing me backwards. After being pushed back, two dolphins appeared on each side of me, and I grabbed hold of their fins as they quickly pulled me forward. This was more than fun! It was exhilarating! Larry and I also enjoyed holding a pole while the dolphins gracefully leaped over it.

Cancer does not exist in moments like this.

Chapter 29 The Sunshine State

Pure bliss.

After the structured swim, Larry and I participated in the natural swim. During the natural swim, we wore snorkeling gear (mask and fins) while swimming with the bottlenose dolphins. Larry and I were instructed not to touch the dolphins during this swim, but instead were encouraged to swim alongside them or dive underwater with them. The instructors said the dolphins are very curious, noticing any differences on human bodies, like scars, tattoos, or amputations. Larry and I must have aroused their curiosity, because they remained very close at all times. Larry commented that swimming with the dolphins had been the most unforgettable experience so far, and I agreed. And now it could be crossed off the bucket list.

Swimming with dolphins—a bucket list adventure.

The bed and breakfast served a hearty poolside breakfast every morning. For the next several days, immediately after breakfast, Larry and I toured the island on rented bicycles. Outings included shopping on Duval Street, climbing the Key Largo lighthouse, visiting the Southern-most House in the United States, and watching sunsets on the beach.

Before returning to St. Petersburg, Larry and I drove through Everglades National Park, the only place in the world where alligators and crocodiles coexist. Larry and I reminisced about all the national parks we had seen so far. The diversity, the uniqueness, the individual beauty of each park was truly amazing. We marveled at God's creation. If so much beauty could be seen here, heaven is beyond my comprehension.

While in St. Petersburg, another bucket list adventure had been accomplished. At John's Pass, Larry and I signed up for a double parasail adventure with Eagle Parasailing. During this excursion, we talked and

Chapter 29 The Sunshine State

laughed while soaring like eagles. Mostly, he and I cherished the quiet stillness. High in the air the noisy boat or laughing spectators on the beach could not be heard. An anonymous writer wrote, "Life is not measured by the number of breaths we take, but by the moments that take our breath away." I cherished moments like this—moments that took my breath away.

I cherished moments like this—moments that took my breath away.

Living and loving life.

Another adventure on the bucket list included an early morning drive to Sanibel Island. Larry loved searching for seashells, and this was an ideal location because Sanibel Island extends far into the Gulf of Mexico, making it a seashell haven. While Larry gathered shells, I photographed the Sanibel lighthouse or Point Ybel Light, the first lighthouse on Florida's Gulf Coast north of Key West. While Larry was wading waist deep in the ocean, I spotted a dolphin behind him swimming along the shoreline.

Before leaving Florida, Larry had one last request. He wanted to visit with his friend, Paul Davidson, who lived in Sarasota. Paul was a good friend and former manager at Larry's FedEx station in Urbana, Illinois. Paul had received news in regards to Larry's cancer through former employees at FedEx. He actively followed Larry's story on Caring Bridge. Paul and Larry arranged to meet at the Sarasota Marina. Paul, Larry, and I enjoyed lunch together under a cabana and afterwards took a stroll around the marina.

Larry with Paul Davidson, friend and former coworker, in Sarasota, Florida.

On Friday, February 25, 2011, I posted the following on Caring Bridge:

> Hello friends and family! It has been awhile since we gave you an update, but our last few days in Florida were very busy. We enjoyed our time here and could not have asked for better weather. We are

Chapter 29 The Sunshine State 111

currently in Arlington, Texas, spending the weekend with Larry's sister, Ann, and her family. We will leave by plane at 6:00 a.m. on Sunday morning to arrive in San Diego where we will board our Hawaiian cruise ship. We are looking forward to spending time with family and having a relaxing, and warm trip before heading home. We should be home around mid-March. We are not taking the computer with us, but we will give you an update after we return. We will see you soon! God Bless! Larry and Tammy

P.S. Check out our parasailing pictures! It was so much fun!

Chapter 30

Hawaiian Cruise

While Larry and I boarded the Holland cruise ship with Ann and Don, I thought, *What a change in scenery this will be.* Except for a few periodic weeks at home, Larry and I had been on the road traveling for six months nonstop. As the ship weighed anchor, I knew this would most likely be Larry's last vacation. His health was declining. He was tired. With this in mind, I was especially thankful to be with family.

Planning excursions for the four different Hawaiian Islands was exciting. Our itinerary (excluding time at sea) included a swim in a lagoon in Hilo, a visit at Akaka Falls State Park, followed by a tour of the city; a visit to Diamond Head in Honolulu, with time on the beach; a zip line excursion in Kauai, followed up with more beach time; and a coastal scenic drive in a rented Mustang convertible on the road to Hana. Hilo was the only destination in which Don and Ann had a different itinerary from ours.

After spending four days at sea, Larry and I exited the ship, receiving a warm "Aloha," as a local woman placed leis around our necks. It felt nice to walk on land again. The tour van drove a scenic route to the lagoon, our first destination. Larry and I loved the swim in the lagoon. I wanted relaxation for Larry, and he reveled in it. Surprisingly, the tem-

Chapter 30 Hawaiian Cruise

perature in the lagoon varied greatly. One arm would feel very warm, while a leg would feel very cool. The scenery was picturesque. Large black volcanic rocks separated the lagoon from the ocean. While lounging in the lagoon, Larry and I watched the waves crash against the rocks.

A relaxing swim in the lagoon.

Before returning to the cruise ship, the tour van stopped at Akaka Falls State Park, allowing time to explore the waterfall and cave.

Larry and I returned from the excursion early enough to hire a taxi to drive back into town, taking advantage of the remaining few hours on the island. Two ladies from the cruise ship joined us on the trip into town. The two of them were quilters, and they wanted to shop for material. The taxi driver agreed to pick us all up at the same location. The driver handed one of the ladies a business card and said, "Just call when you are ready to be picked up." After shopping in the bay front shops, a stress free day quickly turned into a stressful day. The taxi driver did not respond to the phone call. The departure time was rapidly approaching and minutes mattered. In the distance, the ship was visible, but there clearly was not enough time to walk there. Besides, after Larry's long day, he was extremely tired.

The lady who tried to connect with the taxi driver ran into a store and asked for help locating another taxi. The dispatcher called for another cab, but it didn't look like it was going to make it in time. Boarding was only fifteen minutes away. Just when the situation seemed hopeless, a storeowner who had just closed her shop recognized the ladies and asked, "Don't you need to return to the ship? Do you need help?" This kind woman quickly threw everything she had on her seats into the trunk and urged four strangers to pile in three available seats. She drove her little red car as quickly as she could to the dock. She refused payment for her services, but unbeknownst to her Larry stuck cash in her cup holder. Two men were standing at the gate ready to lift the gangway when Larry and I and the two quilting ladies hurried toward them, just in time. This angel in the little red car was at the right place at the right time.

Dinner conversation focused on gratitude. I do not believe in chance; I believe in divine intervention. God intervened and He was worthy to be praised. In Matthew 6:8, Jesus said, "For your Father knows what you need before you ask him." I love this assurance. God knew what I needed before I even asked. I had needlessly been anxious about missing the ship. This event reassured me that God would be with me during the rough days ahead through Larry's sickness and impending death. The grace of Jesus, and nothing else, would carry me through.

I do not believe in chance; I believe in divine intervention.

Exhausted, Larry and I retired early knowing the next day of hiking in Honolulu would tax Larry to his limits. While at sea, Larry often spent time reading and lounging in a chair. He did not want to participate in physical activities. Larry's fatigue was more apparent than ever. I was preparing myself to have a difficult discussion with him after the cruise. I knew he would not want to stop traveling. He was living life. Oh how I wanted it to continue as much as he did!

Diamond Head is a 760-foot crater that serves as one of Hawaii's most famous landmarks. It is a popular hiking destination with panoramic views of Waikiki's shore. Larry was doing fine on the gradual incline of the hiking trail until the group approached two sets of stairs, totaling 175 steps. Larry said to me, "I can't go any farther. I want you to keep going." I did not want to leave Larry. He promised me he would sit and wait right where he was. I felt terrible that he could not go further, but I knew he would feel worse if I stayed behind, so I continued on with the group.

Chapter 30 Hawaiian Cruise

Hesitantly, I walked the remaining steps to the top of the crater. The view Larry did not see was spectacular. I treasure the picture I took of the lighthouse at the top of the crater. I was only able to get this picture because Larry insisted I go on. Larry and I were together all the time. I did not like being separated from him so I quickly hurried back to where he was waiting. This brief separation was a foretaste of the future.

Diamond Head Lighthouse on the eastern end of Waikiki Beach.

Don, Ann, Larry, and I enjoyed lunch and a shopping excursion in Honolulu. Larry was pleased to find a Harley Davidson store where he could purchase a souvenir t-shirt. As dusk approached, the four of us walked to a nearby beach and watched high school aged girls perform the hula. Their graceful moves were enchanting, but the Hawaiian sunset was stunning.

A beautiful Hawaiian sunset.

    Larry's favorite excursion in Hawaii was riding a zip line in Kauai. The trip began with a scenic ride in Backcountry Adventures four-wheel drive vehicle. After gearing up, signing the liability release, and receiving instructions the four of us took turns flying over the rain forest.

    The zip line ended at a bamboo grove with a natural swimming hole. Don does not like heights, but out of love for Larry he decided to join the excursion adventure. This sacrifice meant a lot to Larry. I captured the entire experience, Don's apprehension and Larry's exhilaration, on video and through pictures. Larry's smile was priceless. With this adventure, Larry crossed off another item on his bucket list!

Chapter 30 Hawaiian Cruise

Don, Ann, Tammy, and Larry geared up and ready to go.

Larry on the zip line course at Backcountry Adventures in Kauai.

On the return trip, it rained and Don, who was sitting in the back of the 4x4, got covered with mud. Someone had to do it. Ann and I were concerned about protecting camera equipment so Don gallantly stepped up out of love for his family.

The last group adventure in Hawaii was a drive on the road to Hana. The trip is about the journey as much as the destination. The road winds fifty miles through magnificent seascapes, waterfalls, and botanical gardens. There are fifty-four bridges and six hundred hairpin turns on the road. The road ends at Waianapanapa State Park just on the outskirts of Hana. The beach had gorgeous black sand, sea cliffs, and cobalt-blue water.

Larry drove the rented convertible Mustang on the way there. Ann drove it on the return trip. Due to time constraints, Holland Cruise Line did not sponsor this excursion. A local at the car dealership told Larry to plan on turning around at the halfway point in order to return to the ship on time. I was thrilled when my feet touched the black sand beach in Hana and ecstatic to return to the ship on time.

The return trip to San Diego took four days. While at sea, Ann and I enjoyed the walking deck. Hours passed walking, talking, and breathing in fresh Pacific Ocean air. While Ann and I talked about many things, Larry spoke about the Corvette frequently, and with great zest. Despite his enthusiasm about his new car, Larry fatigued easily, moved slower, and required frequent rest breaks. I knew my adventures with Larry would be ending soon. Soon everything would be a memory. Ann captured this last picture of us on the ship, which I treasure today.

Treasured photo of Larry and Tammy in their Hawaiian attire.

Chapter 31

Rapid Decline

Larry and I returned to Texas with Don and Ann and retrieved the motor home from the storage facility. Larry and I were again on the road, this time returning home to Paxton. I knew Larry still had dreams and plans. So did I, but time would tell how many dreams we still could fulfill. After a couple of days at home, Larry and I flew to Orlando to pick up the Corvette. Larry had great fun driving back to Paxton, and he looked forward to relaxing afternoon drives in his dream vehicle.

Larry wanted to plan the next road trip in the Dutchess to the New England states. I did not see this as being realistic. I did not share my concerns with him though. I knew he had upcoming doctor visits, and tests, and I decided to let the results speak for themselves.

Larry had a CAT scan and lab work completed within two weeks after returning home. On Monday, April 4, 2011, Larry and I received the results. The CAT scan showed Larry's cancer growing at a slower rate. The liver mass increased by 2–3 cm in diameter. However, the liver function was declining rapidly and Dr. Ebert said things would take a turn for the worse at any given time.

On April 7, Larry and I celebrated his dad's birthday with his mom, Brad, and Ann. The family had been unable to get together very often, so this was quite a celebration!

Due to an insurance change at the beginning of the year, it was necessary to find a new internal medicine physician. The insurance company allowed Larry to continue to see his oncologist, Dr. Ebert, for six more months even though he was no longer a preferred provider. Larry and I loved his new primary physician, Dr. Danielle Kim. She was attentive and compassionate. Since Larry was having pain in his lower leg and swelling in his feet and ankles, she ordered a sonogram to make sure he did not have a blood clot. After reviewing Larry's lab work, his hematocrit was 6.7, only 50 percent of normal, so she recommended a blood transfusion, which was scheduled for May 5, 2011.

On Sunday, May 1, 2011, Larry and I drove to Peoria to pick up a new love. Heather Allen, my oldest son's girlfriend, referred Larry and me to someone looking for a new home for their eight-month old Shih Tzu, Zoey. Heather knew I could only have hypo-allergenic animals in the house. The owner of the puppy was now working a twelve-hour shift and could no longer properly care for Zoey. The playful, loving puppy brought new life to our home. Even though getting him adjusted and potty trained was a lot of work, he was a joy to have in the house. Now that Larry and I were spending more time at home, Zoey was a gift from God.

Our new puppy, Zoey.

Chapter 31 Rapid Decline

On Thursday Larry received his scheduled blood transfusion as an outpatient procedure. Thankfully, the leg sonogram the doctor ordered showed no blood clots. Larry received four units of blood, which took about two hours per unit. The following day Larry had a bad headache, but after twenty-four hours he noticed an increase in his energy level. Unfortunately, his short reprieve didn't last long, leaving us to question if it was now time to proceed with the next phase of his care.

Chapter 32

Hospice

I posted the following on Caring Bridge on May 23, 2011:

Sorry for the delay in keeping everyone updated. We have had a busy two weeks as Larry has been having trouble with swelling in his legs and abdomen. Larry's doctor recommended enrollment in hospice and so that is what we have been dealing with the last two weeks. Larry currently has a nurse visit once a week to check his vitals, look for changes, etc. This Wednesday he will be drawing blood so that we do not have to make a trip to Bloomington. Since Larry has had such trouble sleeping (3 to 4 hours a night) and has been very uncomfortable, his doctor has prescribed a sleeping pill and a pain patch. It has helped tremendously! Larry has been sleeping 8 to 10 hours the last couple of nights. Larry and I really appreciate your prayers! God Bless, Larry and Tammy!

Two hospice staff members visited us on the initial visit. The team consisted of an empathetic social worker and a caring nurse. They explained hospice policies and procedures thoroughly. Larry and I were informed that the primary goal of hospice is to improve the quality of a patient's last days. Scott, the hospice nurse, compassionately said, "It

Chapter 32 Hospice

is an honor for us to be in your home and go through this journey with you." I felt confident in their guidance through this difficult time. Larry needed comfort and I needed support. Hospice seemed like a good fit. For Larry, however, enrolling in hospice drove home the point that he would be dying soon. Larry signed the hospice contract on May 13, 2011.

Being Larry's primary caregiver was a monumental commitment. I would be responsible for keeping Larry comfortable and administering the prescribed pain medication. Larry would have periodic visits from hospice staff, but attending to Larry's day-to-day needs fell on my shoulders. While still his wife, I would now be his nurse, his aide, his counselor, and his spiritual mentor. With the hospice team, I would be responsible for assisting my husband to die with dignity. Fortunately, I was not alone. My faith, family, and friends, along with the hospice staff, were there to carry me through this difficult time.

I would be responsible for assisting my husband to die with dignity.

Throughout Larry's illness, I focused on his needs, which naturally resulted in fatigue as I pushed my own needs aside. I was thankful for the emotional, social, and spiritual support that the hospice staff provided, because I realized that I had needs too. Hospice provided trained volunteers to give caregivers respite time. Even though I was fully aware of this service, I did not accept it. Larry might die in my absence and that would be unacceptable to me. Death was inevitable, but the date or time of its occurrence was unknown. Larry made few personal demands of me, but he asked me repeatedly to make sure I would be by his side when he died. I earnestly wanted to honor this wish.

There were many sleepless nights. I was in tune with Larry's breathing pattern so much so that I would immediately waken whenever the breathing became shallow. There was a rhythmic heavy breathing followed by shallow breathing. Neither sounded good, but it was the shallow breathing that frightened me the most. The shallow breathing reminded me of the valley of death. God did not intend for anyone to die, or for loved ones to witness a death. As I listened to Larry's raspy breathing, realizing he would likely die soon, I was thankful that Christ, through His sacrifice, had conquered death. I knew death would occur when Larry's shallow breathing completely stopped.

On a sleepless night, while listening to Larry's shallow breathing, I was suddenly alarmed. There was complete silence. Silence that lasted too long! The rhythm I had been accustomed to was gone. Larry didn't sleep well, nor did I, so I did not want to wake him up if he was in a deep sleep. Instead, I sat up in bed, leaned over, and closely looked to see if his chest was moving. I was uncertain, so I leaned right in front of his face at which point he woke up startled and yelled, "What are you doing?"

"I'm sorry, Larry," I said. "You scared me. I couldn't hear you breathe."

"Well, you scared me!" he said.

In the middle of a sleepless night, Larry and I had a good laugh.

Larry had difficulty walking up the stairs. There were no bedrooms on the first floor, and the couch would not be a comfortable place for him to rest. Hospice recommended a hospital bed, but Larry was not on board with the idea. He didn't like the thought of rearranging the dining room, nor did he like the idea of constantly being reminded of his impending death in a hospital bed.

Larry could be stubborn at times, and I realized he would have to decide on his own if and when he needed the hospital bed. One evening while walking slowly up the stairs he became very short of breath. Once he reached the bedroom, he fell backwards on the bed and his eyes rolled back. I thought I was losing him at that moment. The pain medication was in the house, but hospice had not yet instructed me on how to administer the morphine. I was concerned that I would watch Larry struggle for his last breath, and it was a heart-wrenching thought. I repeatedly asked him if he was okay. After three or four minutes, he finally became coherent. When I thought he was stable enough, I went downstairs and called hospice. The on-call staff member gently walked me through the instructions for administering the morphine. I now had the bottle and syringe easily accessible for use when needed.

Larry and I both enjoyed visits from the hospice staff. Once a week Scott would take Larry's vitals and the two of them would have discussions about anything except cancer. Scott even surprised Larry with a Dairy Queen milkshake on a few occasions. During one of Scott's visits, he said, "Can I give you some advice?"

"Sure," Larry replied.

"It's a nice day. I think you two should take the Corvette out for a country drive."

Larry agreed, and soon he and I were driving slowly on country roads near Paxton with the roof down, savoring the moment. There was something poignant about the drive, and I found myself opening up to my husband. "Larry," I said, "you know I love words. If I could only choose one word to describe you, I would pick the world 'loyal.' You are the most loyal person I know."

This clearly touched and pleased Larry. He flashed his big smile back at me, and said, "Well, if I had to choose one word for you, it would be 'compassionate.' You are the most compassionate person I know."

Later, Scott told me that he was driving home from work that day and saw the two of us on the road. "It choked me up," he said.

On a home visit, after visiting with Larry, Elizabeth, the hospice social worker, broached the subject of funeral arrangements with me. While sitting outside the house, she met with me one on one to discuss funeral planning. She asked if I had made any arrangements, and I told her I had not. She kindly but firmly said, "Tammy, it is time to start thinking about that."

I agreed with Elizabeth. I needed her prompting. I knew death was near. I knew there were many details to address and plan. I often would make up excuses to avoid making decisions. I would tell myself, "You are busy as Larry's caretaker. You are so fatigued. You need to spend as much time with him as you can." I was not in denial about losing Larry. The end was approaching, and I needed to begin making preparations.

Despite the definite progression of multiple effects that cancer was having on Larry and me, there were things the disease could not touch. Cancer could not shake Larry's faith in God or love for me. Every day he woke up with a positive attitude. He frequently expressed gratitude to me and to others for the smallest acts of kindness. He didn't complain and seldom ever expressed any self-pity.

I know how hard and extremely difficult this decision was for him.

As the trips down the stairs to the restroom grew more and more difficult, and after the fainting incident, Larry finally agreed to have the hospital bed delivered. I know how hard and extremely difficult this decision was for him. I did not want the hospital bed any more than he did. This would be the first time that we would not be sleeping together in the same bed since getting married. It would be harder for me to know if he became short of breath. I stayed as close as I could on a couch near his bed.

As a caretaker, I found the hospice book, *Gone From My Sight, the Dying Experience* by Barbara Karnes, RN, very helpful. She states, "Each person approaches death in their own way, bringing to this last experience their own uniqueness. Death is as unique as the individual who is experiencing it." She includes a summary of guidelines, outlining events and symptoms that could frequently be seen at specified time intervals prior to death. For instance, I noticed Larry becoming more withdrawn, and this was out of character for him. Karnes states that within one to three months prior to death, patients sometimes withdraw from the world and people. This helped me to not take it so personally. It gave me a better perspective. Larry was preparing for his life to end. Was I?

Larry did not like staying in the house. He said, "I am tired of staring at the same four walls." He wanted to go visit Brad in Indiana. I was not keen on this idea and voiced my concerns with him and with other family members. However, Scott talked me through possible scenarios and helped to make Larry's desire a reality.

Chapter 33

Last Road Trip

After arriving in Indiana, Brad, Deb, Larry and I went to dine at one of Larry's favorite restaurants. He loved Golden Corral because of the vast choices offered on their buffet. Larry was pleased to walk through the line and fill his plate with many of his favorite foods. However, when he sat down to eat, the mood at the table quickly changed. Larry took just a few bites, put down his fork, and said, "I'm going to wait for you in the car." He wanted to eat a meal with family, but he was losing ground fast, and he knew it.

Before Larry and I left Indiana, he wanted to get into Brad and Deb's swimming pool. He struggled to get onto the air mattress. Brad offered to assist him, but Larry was determined to do it on his own. His legs were swollen and his arms were weak, but he finally accomplished what he set out to do. I had quit taking many pictures at this point. It was just too painful. I wanted photographs that would tell Larry's story, but I did not want the story to end. Larry's declining health was obvious in the pictures. Soon pictures and memories would be all I could hold in my hands and my heart. "Larry, can I take your picture?" I asked. Too tired to smile, he answered me with a wave.

Therapeutic pool time for Larry.

I posted the picture of Larry in the pool on his Caring Bridge website. On June 20, 2011, Debb Rhyce, a new friend, replied in the guestbook with the following comment:

> I am happy to hear Larry had some much needed pool time! There is nothing like relaxing and floating in a swimming pool to make you feel better. Ever since we met you two in Utah, you have been an inspiration to me. God has a plan for each of us, and I believe meeting you both has made a difference in my life. You guys have touched more people than you know. We will keep you in our prayers.

Chapter 34

World's Coolest Dad

I received a phone call from Travis and Tyler on June 19, 2011. It was Father's Day, and the two of them wanted to drive to Paxton to visit Larry. I knew Larry would be touched by their visit, but I needed to prepare the boys for when they saw him. I told them he looked gaunt and his body was frail. I tried to prepare them as best as I could. Each day I watched Larry deteriorate, but for others the interval changes could be shocking. Cancer was destroying my husband's body, but not his spirit. Larry still smiled. Larry still loved. Larry still had faith and hope.

Tyler and Travis brought Larry a t-shirt for Father's Day that said "World's Coolest Dad." I wanted Larry to wear the shirt for a group picture, but I did not ask him to change since his body was so frail.

Travis and Tyler realized this would most likely be the last time they would see Larry alive. Before leaving, Tyler said to him, "Why you? It's not fair!"

Larry's response shocked Tyler and left a lasting impression on him. He replied, "Why not me? I'm not afraid to die, and others may need more time."

Tyler was astonished that someone could be so unselfish. Tyler later told me how much this comment affected him.

Travis and Tyler with Larry on Father's Day.

Chapter 35

Acts of Kindness

Larry was eating less and less, and I was thankful when he would eat anything. Usually, instead, he munched on ice all day. I had come home from the store one day with two small bags of ice for Larry. He said, "Why didn't you get a large bag?" I said that it was hard for me to carry a large bag. He said, "I prefer a large bag." His comment didn't make a lot of sense, but in retrospect, I wonder now, if having a large bag present implied that he would be around to finish using it up.

When friends and neighbors, Gary and Margaret, came to visit, they asked if there was anything they could do. I told Gary and Margaret I would really appreciate it if they would bring me a large bag of ice to put in the freezer. Not only did Gary and Margaret do this, the two of them made a decision to do something special for Larry. Knowing he liked to be outside, they hired a contractor to install a heavy-duty railing on the back porch. Gary and Margaret completed this project knowing Larry would not be able to use the railing for long. This railing also allowed Larry's mother, who had difficulty going up the back stairs, to come and visit him more easily.

Larry kept telling me he needed a haircut. My sister, Heather, a beautician, wanted to visit us. Heather and her husband, Chris, made the trip on Sunday, June 26, 2011. Prior to leaving their home in Hudson, Illinois, Heather made a lemon meringue pie for Larry—another act of kindness and love! Lemon meringue pie was Larry's favorite, and he would have enjoyed every bite of it if he could have eaten it. Unfortunately, on that Sunday morning Larry began having trouble swallowing. He couldn't eat a single bite. Heather was, however, able to cut Larry's hair in the kitchen. A simple act of kindness that made Larry very happy. As sick as he was, he took pride in being well groomed.

On Monday Larry had two visitors. In the morning, Scott stopped by to check his vitals. Scott gave him instructions on how to swallow. He encouraged him to drink an Ensure protein drink as often as possible. "It is enough to sustain your life," he said. He instructed Larry to tip his head forward to open up his esophagus so that he wouldn't choke. Scott said he would be stopping by more often.

Pastor Clonch from the Bloomington/Normal Seventh-day Adventist Church also came to visit Larry. Pastor Clonch was my former pastor, but he also had pastored Larry's church in Champaign years before. Pastor Clonch had prayer with Larry and left him with several pamphlets. The pamphlet that caught my attention was, "Facing Death Without Fear."

While Larry was napping, Pastor Clonch met with me in the kitchen. I shared my thoughts about the order of the service with him. Pastor Clonch gave me his input and typed the following schedule as he and I spoke:

Memorial Service: Larry Allan Smestad

I Hotel, Champaign, IL

Date and Time (TBA)

Music Prelude and Slide Show (looping)	
Welcome and Opening Prayer	Pastor Ray Plummer
Eulogy	Pastor Ray Plummer
Special Music	"Amazing Grace" Penny Matthews
Lighting Candles	Ann King and Brad Smestad
Poem	Lisa Edelbach

Chapter 35 Acts of Kindness

Sharing Time	Ken Hauser (FedEx)
	Tyler Kern
	Tammy Smestad
Message of Comfort	Pastor Larry Clonch
Larry's Life Journey (Pictures/Video)	Tyler Kern and Tammy Smestad
Benediction	Pastor Larry Clonch
Instrumental Postlude	

My life, the life I loved, the life I had become accustomed to, had drastically changed. In just three years I went from planning a wedding to planning a memorial service—joy to sorrow.

After Pastor Clonch left, I sat with Larry while he napped. I noticed he had moved the pamphlet on facing death. When Larry woke, I glanced at the pamphlet and asked Larry if he wanted to talk about it. He said, "No." There was no need to discuss this subject. Larry had a strong, Biblical understanding about death. He had no fear in dying. Larry grasped the hope and promise of eternal life.

June 28, 2011, was Larry's mother's birthday. He, like me, wanted everything to be like it once was. Early in the morning, Larry said, "I want to take my mother out to dinner for her birthday." The desire and will were present, though Larry knew it could not and would not happen. If Larry were to see his mother on her birthday, she had to come to him. And that is what she did.

As a mother myself, I wanted to give Larry and his mother time alone. I soon would be a widow, but Mom Smestad was losing a son for the second time. She'd had no last words with her son Rick, who died unexpectedly. With Larry there was an opportunity to speak and share love between mother and son. For many weeks I had not left my home to run errands. I walked to the bank and post office while Larry and his mother visited. What was said and what took place was between them. What I do know is how much Larry loved and treasured his mother.

Chapter 36

Unexpected Blessings

    Like Monday, April 19, 2010, Wednesday, June 29, 2011, is a day I will never forget. Early in the morning I quickly showered and dressed. Simple tasks that removed me from Larry's presence created stress. Larry desired to have me by his side when he died, and I was determined to honor his request. The thought of his death was always on my mind. When would it happen? Would it happen suddenly or with warning?

    When I opened the bathroom door, I was surprised to see Larry sitting on the edge of his hospital bed. I was more surprised when he opened his arms wide and said, "Come here." At 5'2", when I approached Larry, he and I were at eye level. Larry looked intensely into my eyes, and I into his. Larry's eyes revealed his attributes of strength, loyalty, and compassion. He wrapped his arms tightly around me. My husband and I shared the longest embrace. I had not seen this vigor in Larry for months. His endurance amazed me. He held me tightly until I released my emotional pain. I began to quiver. I held him tightly as I cried and cried some more. Through my sobbing, I said what was on my mind. "Larry, I know I am going to lose you, but I will so look forward to seeing you again!"

    Lisa, Larry's niece, and her entire family drove from Michigan to visit Larry Wednesday afternoon. Carle Medical Supply had previously

Chapter 36 Unexpected Blessings

delivered an oxygen tank, which seemed to help Larry tremendously, but I was still concerned about his fatigue. He needed frequent naps, and I was prepared to speak on Larry's behalf, cutting the visit short, if need be. I knew his family would understand.

Larry's perseverance throughout the day astonished me. For hours, Larry talked, laughed, and shared. This was unusual. I was happy, but confused. While smiling, talking, and sitting up in bed, Larry had simple requests. He asked me to bring him his metal car collection from the sunroom. He smiled broadly as he handed out cars to his young niece and nephews to remember him by.

Laura and Sarah, daughters of Larry's brother Brad, live close by in Champaign. With their husbands, they visited with Larry as well. Larry enjoyed and cherished this time spent with family.

I never expected what took place next.

I never expected what took place next. While the family was seated around Larry's bed, he nonchalantly said to me, "Tammy, will you go into the sunroom? In the second drawer there is a small wooden box. Will you please bring it to me?" I was shocked at his request. I knew the drawer was full of pictures, cards, and envelopes. I had never seen a small wooden box in that drawer or anywhere in the home.

God impressed on my heart what I would find in the drawer. I know some people would be understandably skeptical about this, but I am convinced that God placed the box in the drawer and revealed to Larry where it was when his niece was in our home and the timing was just right for Larry to present the ring to her.

I gently handed the box to Larry. His smile lit up the room. Relatives were puzzled as Larry gently opened the lid. His hand delicately picked up the long lost ruby ring. He turned and admired it in his hand. He then extended his hand to his niece, Laura, and with a smile said, "I am keeping my promise." Laura's response pierced my heart. She did not cry. She wailed. I now had a better understanding of the biblical term "wailing."

Friends from church, Gary and Lisa Babb, also dropped by for a short visit. It was getting rather late as friends and family gathered around Larry. Larry's niece and her family planned to return to Michigan that evening. Larry sensed how difficult it was for his family to leave. I believe this is why Larry said, "I want to pray before anyone leaves." Larry prayed for safe travels for his family. Then, encircling his bed, holding hands, family and friends prayed for Larry.

Larry was tired, but not extremely fatigued as he often was. After the house emptied, we talked briefly about the highlights of the day. I expected he would sleep soundly, and I told Larry I wouldn't welcome visitors the following day. I said, "I think you'll be even more tired tomorrow." I kissed him goodnight as he quickly drifted to sleep. While Larry closed his eyes, he said, "I'll wake you, if ..."

How could I sleep soundly when death could occur at any time? What if Larry could not speak? What if I didn't realize he was taking his last breath? As hard as death would be to witness, I worried even more about not being at his side.

Chapter 37

Too Long

Another day dawned. My life with Larry had turned upside down, but the sun still rose on Thursday morning, June 30, 2011. Larry woke exhausted and short of breath. What a difference from the day before. I asked him if he could drink an Ensure, and he said, "I'll try." It took over an hour for him to get one small drink down. Surprisingly, he then asked for a popsicle. This was my husband's breakfast, lunch, and dinner. Due to his weakness and difficulty swallowing, his food options were limited to strawberry, chocolate, or vanilla Ensure and multi-flavored popsicles.

After eating Larry wanted to go back to sleep. He said, "I'm tired."

"I knew you would be after your long day yesterday," I replied. I told Larry I would wait to take my shower until after he woke from his nap. I sat on a stool at the kitchen island working on my computer while Larry slept. Larry's birthday was only a week away. I had started on a project I wanted to complete before that date. Larry made me promise to not buy him any presents. He said, "It is pointless." He did not say I could not make him a gift. I wanted this present to be a gift of love, a gift of hope for Larry.

My idea was to create an inspirational DVD from the beautiful nature pictures we had collected while traveling. I searched for Bible verses and promises that correlated with each picture. On a picture of a lighthouse in Alaska, I wrote, "God is our refuge and strength, a very present help in trouble." Another one, "He will guide them and lead them beside springs of water," was placed on a picture of a beautiful waterfall. The DVD began with pictures from the honeymoon in Alaska and ended with pictures from the last trip, the Hawaiian cruise. I knew Larry would enjoy the pictures and scripture readings while the beautiful melody of "How Great is the Lord" played in the background. Most of all, I wanted Larry to be encouraged and empowered with Bible promises. God had blessed us so much. He was worthy to be praised.

While I worked on the project in the kitchen, I had my eyes on Larry. If he moved, I noticed. I watched him get out of bed and walk a short distance to the bathroom. I anticipated he would immediately go back to sleep when he returned. Larry did not like being dependent. I understood. If the roles were reversed, I would not like it either. I often stepped in to assist Larry, but he seemed to prefer that I wait until he asked. After several minutes had passed, I became uneasy, but I rationalized that he probably needed just a little more time. Suddenly, I had a sick feeling in my stomach. My brain screamed, *It's been too long!*

My brain screamed, *It's been too long!*

With a sense of dread, I walked the short distance from the kitchen, through the dining room, and past Larry's bed. My right hand was on the doorknob as I called out to Larry. With knots in my stomach, I called out again, "Larry. Larry, are you okay?" There was no answer, just silence.

I tried to open the door, but Larry's right foot was in the way. He was sitting on the stool with his hands folded on his lap and his head bowed, in a praying position. I reached out to him through the small opening in the door and wailed, "Larry! No, God! Larry!" I touched him and tried to wake him, but he was gone. I had been kneeling on the floor but now sat down by the door. I wrapped my arms around my legs, leaned forward, and wailed. The day before I had heard Larry's niece wail when he gave her the ring. Now it was my turn! I knew I should call hospice and family members, but I needed this moment. I was so distraught. I was supposed to be with him when he died. I should have been holding his hand and telling him I loved him. This was not how I envisioned losing him. But, as Barbara Karnes had warned, "Death is an unknown and unique experience."

Chapter 37 Too Long

Hospice was the first call I made. I don't remember to whom I spoke, but the woman on the phone said, "I am so sorry. I will notify Scott."

Scott called me immediately, expressing sympathy. He said, "Tammy, I am changing my schedule for the day. I will be at your home soon."

While waiting for Scott, I called Brad and asked him to contact everyone on his side of the family. I also called my mother and asked her to contact my family as well. I called Travis and Tyler to tell them the news myself. There were many other names written on a list that I needed to contact. In between phone calls, I knelt beside the door, reaching to touch Larry. I kept repeating, "I am so sorry, Larry!"

When Scott arrived I quickly opened the door to lead him directly to Larry. Much to my surprise, Scott stood still. He extended his arms wide. Scott knew Larry was gone. With deep concern, he addressed my needs. I welcomed his embrace, just as I had Larry's the day before. Through my tears, I said to Scott, "I didn't get to say goodbye."

Compassionately, Scott said, "Tammy, you've been saying goodbye all along. I have seen nothing but love in this home." I understood what Scott was telling me, but I could not escape the disturbing thought that I had not fulfilled Larry's final wishes.

Together Scott and I walked to the bathroom. He, like me, was hesitant to move Larry's foot. I knew Scott would feel terrible if Larry fell off the toilet, but he needed to do his job. Scott held on to Larry's shoulder with his left hand as he moved Larry's foot just enough to open the door. Scott began talking to Larry while in the bathroom. The night before, after everyone had left, Larry had asked me to bring him a clean t-shirt. Ironically, when he died he was wearing a Harley t-shirt that said, "I could give up, but I'm not a quitter." I heard Scott softly say to his friend and patient, "You are right, buddy. You were not a quitter."

After a short pause, Scott said, "11:18 a.m." I knew he was pronouncing the time of death. Scott said to me, "God sure loved Larry. He took him quickly." Scott knew I was agonizing over Larry's last minutes. Scott again said, "A major organ ruptured, and Larry went fast." Scott needed to move Larry from the awkward position he was in. He asked for my permission to lay him on the large rug in the bathroom. I told him that would be fine. The house, unfortunately, had only one bathroom. Anyone who needed to use the bathroom would be alone in the room with Larry.

The phone rang constantly. Brad had an overnight bag packed waiting for this call. He was already on the road. Tyler called to tell me he was on his way as well. Scott said, "Tammy, you will have until about 4:00 p.m. for anyone who wants to view Larry." Larry had asked to be cremated, but I had not made any arrangements yet. I asked Scott to talk to Elizabeth to see if she could help make the arrangements.

Elizabeth was as kindhearted as Scott. When she had prompted me earlier to begin making arrangements, she had also informed me about grief support services offered through hospice. I was very interested in the *Life After Loss* program. The empathy and compassion shown by Scott and Elizabeth made me want to consider volunteer work with hospice someday. I had walked this journey for a reason. I felt God impressing on my heart the desire to assist other grieving families.

Larry would be in the home for just a few more hours before being transferred to the mortuary. The departure felt so final. Many family members were on their way to say their last goodbyes. I was thankful Elizabeth made phone calls and arrangements, allowing me time with Larry and our family.

When family and friends called, it was emotionally draining to keep repeating the story. In between calls, Scott asked me if I was drinking water. "Tammy, it is so important for you to keep yourself hydrated," he said. I knew he was right, and I appreciated his concern for me.

Scott sat quietly on the couch working on his computer while I cried and talked on the phone. When asked how I was doing, I didn't know how to respond. How should I be doing? I had just lost my husband. I didn't know if my behavior and reactions were normal or abnormal. I felt relief. I felt guilt. I felt a great loss.

I turned to Scott, and asked, "Scott, how am I doing?" If anyone knew the answer, it would be him.

"Tammy, you are doing great," he said. "I am really proud of you."

Family members started to arrive, and I was relieved to see them. I needed to share my sorrow with them and vice versa. I understood the importance and value of just being present. Sympathetic words were exchanged, and there were times of silence. One by one family members entered the bathroom and closed the door. Sometimes a wail or cry could be heard through the wall or sometimes when the door was opened. No one cried alone. Pain and sorrow were shared.

Brad was the last to arrive. In fact, he arrived just minutes before the mortician. After Brad greeted family and was introduced to Scott, he was the last to say goodbye to Larry. Scott calmly approached me and said, "Tammy, it is time. I would appreciate it if you and your family would step outside in the backyard." I asked him why and he explained. Scott said moving a deceased loved one can be a rather traumatic experience. "I want to spare you and your family," Scott said. "You will have one last opportunity to view Larry."

Chapter 37 Too Long

Brad was the only family member who stayed inside. I don't know if he offered his services or was asked, but it was Brad's character to give assistance. The mortician was a woman, and I am sure she appreciated Scott and Brad's help. I imagined it would be difficult to lift Larry's body onto the gurney.

A line formed outside on the sidewalk. My eyes were focused on the back door of my home. Soon my husband would be rolled out and carried down the steps, permanently exiting the home he and I had shared—a home filled with love. The only comforting thought in the midst of my grieving was that God had carried me through the past and He would faithfully carry me through the future.

Scott was right. Seeing Larry zipped in a body bag on a gurney was hard to witness. The mortician stopped on the sidewalk where I was standing. The bag was unzipped just enough to see Larry's face. I gave my husband a kiss for the very last time and looked away. I struggled with Larry leaving and with the thought of cremation.

Chapter 38

Memorial Plans

I was grateful Tyler and Amelia offered to stay with me for a few days. I needed their help, and I appreciated their presence. I was fatigued, distraught, and confused. Having assistance in making decisions and planning Larry's memorial was a blessing. Amelia jumped right in, cleaning out the refrigerator and making room for food that was being delivered. Tyler searched through family videotapes, gathering any footage he could of Larry. Tyler and Amelia both went with me to an appointment to reserve a room at the Illini Hotel in Champaign for Larry's memorial service. We estimated that over 200 people would attend, so we needed a large room.

Preparing Larry's memorial service was my new focus. I wanted it to be very special. I wanted to honor Larry's life and all that he stood for. I gathered and scanned pictures while Tyler continued working on the DVD. I completed my DVD project that I wanted to give Larry as a gift. My plan was to have the DVD with scripture and nature pictures looping before the service. Tyler let me view his progress on the DVD he was creating until he got to the end, at which point he said, "I am doing something that I want to surprise you with." He does exceptional work, so I trusted his judgment.

Chapter 38 Memorial Plans

Larry was gone from sight but reminders of him were everywhere throughout the home. His navy blue and white striped bathrobe was draped over a chair in the dining room near where his bed had been. Eyeglasses were on the bathroom counter where Larry had removed them to wash his face. A favorite gel pen he had held in his hand was lying on top of an uncompleted crossword puzzle. His Bible, with Larry Smestad engraved on the leather cover, was on the coffee table.

Seeing these reminders of Larry prompted me to gather them to showcase at the memorial service. Unread books and uncompleted crossword puzzles reminded me of the fragility of life. Amelia enjoys decorating, so I asked her if she would be in charge of setting up the display tables. I gathered items such as Larry's prayer quilt, the bucket list, his Bible, special t-shirts, books, personalized license plates, and of course, many pictures.

Brad went with me to Renner-Wikoff Chapel to prepare the obituary for the newspaper. The following words were drafted for my approval:

Obituary: Larry A. Smestad

PAXTON – Larry A. Smestad, 58, of Paxton died at 11:18 a.m. Thursday (June 30, 2011) at home.

A memorial service will be held from 2 to 4 p.m. July 10 at the I Hotel, Champaign, in the Illinois Ballroom.

Larry Allan Smestad was born July 7, 1952, in Breckenridge, Minn., a son of Blair and Lois Danielson Smestad. He married Tammy Singer-Kern on Oct. 25, 2008, in Champaign. She survives.

He is survived by his mother; two stepsons, Travis Kern, Mackinaw, and Tyler Kern, Deer Creek; a sister, Ann King, Arlington, Texas; a brother, Brad Smestad, Princeton, Ind.; four nieces; and a nephew.

He was preceded in death by a brother, Rick Smestad, and a nephew.

Larry worked as a courier for FedEx for 27 years. He was a member of the Champaign Seventh-day Adventist Church.

Condolences may be offered at www.renner-wikoffchapel.com.

I approved the obituary for print and didn't realize until much later that Larry's dad was not mentioned as a surviving parent.

While at the funeral home, I chose a beautiful tan and crème marbled urn. I searched through examples of memorial announcements. The cardstock for the announcement was an easy choice. I chose a white cardstock with an off-white border, which would frame Larry's picture. I read through poems, quotes, and Bible verses popularly chosen for memorial or funeral services. The examples were good, but too familiar. I wanted something different and more personal. I only had a few days to finalize my plans. The funeral home needed ample time to print over 200 announcements.

Ten days is not a lot of time to plan and organize this type of event. Time spent shopping for attire, candles, and flowers, and making decisions about the funeral service kept me from tending to details like writing my speech. Small details were time consuming. I regretted not putting more thought and effort into planning the service prior to his death.

I turned to the Internet for inspiration to complete Larry's memorial card and found a compilation of short four-line poems to personalize and customize Larry's announcement at Frans Candles. The poetic words I chose summarized the tears and memories left behind. The words spoke of Larry's faithful journey and hope of eternity:

>Our thoughts are ever with you
>
>Though you have passed away.
>
>And those who loved you dearly
>
>Are thinking of you today.
>
>We can't have old days back
>
>When we were all together.
>
>But secret tears and loving thoughts
>
>Will be with us forever.
>
>We all have different journeys,
>
>Different paths along the way.
>
>We are all meant to learn some things,
>
>But never meant to stay.
>
>Life is but a stopping place,
>
>A pause in what's to be.

Chapter 38 Memorial Plans

> A resting place along the road,
>
> To sweet eternity.

Initially, I struggled with the thought of cremating Larry's body. It was hard for me to put my concerns into words. I had shared with Larry the sadness and uneasiness I felt when I attended my grandfather's memorial service many years ago. I had not seen my grandfather for years since he had moved to Arizona, and I was extremely uncomfortable at his service, staring at an urn. Unlike Larry, I processed death and loss better by viewing a body. This is why I desired to spend as much time as I could with Larry on the day of his death.

Chapter 39

Bringing Larry Home

On July 7, 2011, I received a phone call from Renner-Wikoff Chapel informing me that Larry's urn and printed materials were ready for pick up. I am sure they did not realize this was the date of his birthday. I had been anticipating their call. The day of his birthday was a hard day, but much to my surprise, I looked forward to bringing Larry's urn home.

With thoughts racing through my mind and butterflies in my stomach, I drove to the funeral home. After handing the mortician my final payment, she presented me with a box of printed material. She also gave me a nice bag holding the t-shirt Larry had worn on the day of his death. I was appreciative she honored my request to save the shirt he was wearing, but I did not realize how difficult it would be to see the shirt again. Everything seemed to be difficult now.

The mortician said, "If you want to carry these items, I will carry the urn for you. It is rather heavy."

I replied, "If you don't mind, I would like to carry the urn myself." I was ready to wrap my arms around the beautiful marble urn encasing Larry's remains. My grasp was firm and I was confident in my strength and ability to carefully carry it to the car. I wanted to place the urn on the passenger seat beside me, but during my drive to the funeral home I

Chapter 39 Bringing Larry Home

had decided the floor would be the safest place to transport it. For three unforgettable years, I was in the passenger seat. Larry had safely driven me through God's beautiful country creating lasting memories. I was now in the driver's seat. My partner in making decisions was gone. With my right hand, I grasped the top of Larry's urn, holding it steady on the drive home.

There are two strong wooden bookshelves on the main floor in my home. I walk by them many times a day. I cleared off two of the shelves, choosing this space for Larry's urn since the open rooms were where I spent most of my day. After the service I planned to place pictures and several of the display items on the shelf surrounding Larry's urn.

> *My life had been turned upside down and everything was different, once again.*

I was astonished at how comfortable and peaceful I felt having the urn in my presence. I liked the thought of not having to drive to a cemetery. Though it seemed odd in a way, it was comforting to have Larry's remains in my home. My life had been turned upside down and everything was different, once again. I did, however, experience peace in knowing Larry's wishes had been honored. Peace, a precious gift from God.

In three short days the memorial service would take place. Tyler forwarded me a draft of his speech. I was grateful he allowed me to read it in advance. I appreciated that he valued my opinion, but mostly, I knew the reading would be very emotional. I cried as I read each line. I knew I would cry again when I heard him speak at the service, but it was helpful for me to have private time to process his thoughts.

Chapter 40

Memorial Service

On Sunday afternoon, July 10, 2011, family and friends gathered to honor Larry's memory. Larry's good friend Billy Hayden and his sweet wife, Rachel, with whom Larry and I attended church, greeted guests at the door while handing attendees Larry's memorial card. Upon entering the room, Ellen again greeted guests while asking them to sign the memorial book. Near Ellen, in the back corner of the room were the two display tables showcasing a few of Larry's belongings. As planned, visitors watched the nature and scripture DVD on two large screens as guests were seated.

Chapter 40 Memorial Service 149

Larry's Bible, prayer quilt, and pictures on the display table.

Larry's unfinished crossword puzzle and glasses on the display table.

Pastor Plummer from the Champaign Seventh-day Adventist Church welcomed friends and family and opened the memorial service with prayer. He then shared the eulogy. Larry's urn was placed on a beautiful wood table directly in front of the landing where the speakers spoke. Beautiful flower arrangements and plants delivered by family and friends framed each side of the urn. A poster-size picture of Larry was placed on an easel on the right side of the table.

Penny Matthews sang Chris Tomlin's updated version of the John Newton classic, "Amazing Grace." Larry and I loved this song. The song had personal meaning, as we had reveled in God's amazing grace. Penny had sung at our wedding, and now she was singing at Larry's memorial.

Chapter 40 Memorial Service

After Penny's special music, Larry's oldest niece, Lisa, from Michigan, read a poem written by an unknown author. Brad and Ann each lit a candle while Lisa spoke:

> Those we love remain with us
>
> For love itself lives on.
>
> And cherished memories never fade
>
> Because a loved one's gone.
>
> Those we love can never be
>
> More than a thought apart.
>
> For as long as there is memory,
>
> They'll live on in the heart.

This poem captured how I felt. While death physically separated me from Larry, there were two things death could not do. Death could not take away my memories, and death could not take away my love. Larry will live on in my heart and in the hearts of all the lives he touched.

Ken Hauser, manager at FedEx, spoke of Larry's twenty-seven years of service to the company. "Larry was a dedicated and loyal employee," Ken said. Ken said FedEx colleagues would be wearing purple ribbons with Larry's name and badge number for the next month. I was touched and appreciative they were doing this in remembrance of him.

Tyler tearfully gave a very touching speech with an appeal:

> For those of you who haven't met me, I am Larry's stepson. Any son may be skeptical when their mother says they have met someone. When I met Larry he seemed to make my mom happy, which is all I really wanted.
>
> A year later I began warming up to Larry. He was always open for good conversation. He enjoyed being a part of my life and attending my events. I studied video production in college, and they held what would be considered the Oscars of my university. I was honored to have Larry and my mom watching in the audience as I accepted the award for Best Director. Larry and my mom left me a voicemail a few weeks later after I gave them a DVD to watch that I had made. I wish I still had the voicemail today. They told me how proud they both were and how successful they thought I'd be. I always received encouragement from them.

I was out to dinner with Larry and my mom when they got the call that changed their lives drastically. They stepped out of the restaurant to take the call. When they returned they informed me of the horrible situation. Larry had colon cancer.

Larry was beginning to have more and more doctor's appointments. He was at an appointment the day of my college graduation. I told him not to worry about attending, that I knew he wanted to and that was good enough. He insisted on being there. I knew it was nearly impossible for him to come from his doctor's appointment at Mayo Clinic in Minnesota to my college graduation in Normal, Illinois. Sure enough, he made it on time, and I began calling him Superman, because nobody could have gotten there that fast unless they were Superman. I knew it meant a lot for him to be there, and that meant a lot to me.

After I graduated I moved to Nashville, Tennessee. That's when Larry decided to make his bucket list. They bought the RV and started seeing the country. I was happy every time they could fit Nashville into their agenda. They visited me many times down in Tennessee. They even convinced me, and my girlfriend, Amelia, to go on a weeklong trip with them to the beach in Gulf Shores, Alabama. During this experience is when I really bonded with Larry. We both enjoyed walking the beach looking for seashells. Larry took me to Lambert's Café, which is known for their "thrown rolls." It is now my favorite restaurant. Unfortunately, our vacation ended and we all had to go back to our lives.

Larry was always positive. I never heard a complaint about his situation, and he always managed to smile. I moved back to Illinois at the end of May. I wanted to be here this summer to spend time with my family, especially Larry.

I went to visit him when I first moved back. He was eager to take me for a ride in the Corvette convertible. We hopped in the car and drove off. As soon as we got out of town, Larry floored it. My head bobbed back, and I looked over at him and he was smiling, having fun. These are the memories that I will never forget. When we came back, I gave Larry a hug and headed home.

I knew my time with him was almost up. I came back on Father's Day to give Larry his present. I got him a t-shirt that said "World's Coolest Dad." I wanted him to know that I loved him like a dad. He was such a positive person and so much fun to be around.

He heard me say, "Why you, Larry?" when talking about his cancer. Larry was quick to respond. He said, "Why not me? I have a strong relationship with the Lord, why not give someone else

Chapter 40 Memorial Service

more time?" He said, "It's better for someone else who doesn't have a relationship with God to have more time." Tears filled my eyes when we left his house. I couldn't believe how unselfish a person could be. How he would rather it be him than someone else who doesn't believe.

This is why I wanted to speak today. I want you all to know Larry's testimony. We should all learn from Larry. If you have not yet let Jesus into your heart, if you haven't accepted the Lord as your Savior, well guess what … it's not too late. You still have time to build that relationship. Just know that time is precious, and we should not waste it. Life on earth is short, but life in heaven is eternal.

I would like to say a prayer. If you would, please bow your heads.

Dear Lord, thank you for bringing Larry into our lives. Please help us cope with this terrible loss. We know, as we feel sad inside that we are not alone. We can feel Your love with us everywhere we go. We are eagerly awaiting Your arrival, Lord. Please mark a spot in the sky for us to meet up with Larry and be together again in Your grace. In Jesus name we pray, Amen.

I struggled preparing my speech. If I were to speak, and I wanted to, I needed to avoid emotional triggers. Addressing specifics such as Larry's diagnosis or death would be too painful to share. Memories from traveling and pursued dreams on the bucket list would also be triggers. After rewriting my speech several times, I decided to focus on lessons I learned from Larry. My kindhearted brother-in-law, Don, agreed to be my back-up speaker if need be. He had a copy of my speech in his hands. All I needed to do was give him a nod if I needed to have him speak in my place. But I wanted to do this myself, so I avoided even looking Don's way. Prayers gave me the strength to speak.

I thanked family, friends, and coworkers for attending Larry's service. Then, I said:

Larry would be very touched. Instead of sharing my journey with Larry, I decided to focus on lessons I learned from him, and there were many.

First and foremost, Larry lived his faith. He prayed and truly believed if his prayer was answered it was God's will and if it was not it was still God's will. Sometimes, it is hard for us as Christians to wait and trust, but that is what my husband did.

When Larry was given his diagnosis in April of 2010 he was ready to put up a good fight, stating he was a "Swede" and they don't go down easy. One of his best coping mechanisms was his positive thinking. When he was told anything negative in the doctor's office, it was immediately dismissed when we walked out the door. His spirit during this journey, and his "no pity" attitude were amazing to all who knew him.

 Larry and I created lasting memories. We were determined to make each day a memory. The most important things to me are still the small things, such as holding hands when we walked, whether on the beach, or walking the dog. While traveling in the motor home, we experienced beautiful panoramic scenery that took our breath away. Our time together in nature truly nourished our souls!

 Larry felt strongly that this was a pivotal time in his life to be a witness. I am proud Larry accomplished that. Neither one of us had previous experience with public speaking, but we were passionate about encouraging others to make changes in their lifestyle, to strengthen their faith, and to listen to what their bodies were telling them.

 Larry's most endearing quality was loyalty. He was loyal to God, his church, his family, his friends, his job, and his pets. I have personally never met anyone as loyal as my husband. Larry's personal gift to me was the gift of encouragement. When he saw the good in me, or in you, he was quick to acknowledge it. He always complimented. The strength and confidence I now have comes from Larry. Today, I am a much better person having known him and loved him. Walking by his side throughout this journey, I saw firsthand what he was made of—thoughtfulness, strength, and faith!

In addition, I shared with the audience the divine intervention during Larry's last days on earth. I started with the haircut on Sunday, and while holding the wooden box in my hand, I shared how God had revealed to Larry the location of the ruby ring he had so desperately searched for. God had intervened. He allowed Larry to pass the ruby ring to his niece on Wednesday, the day before he died. "God was concerned with the desires of Larry's heart," I said.

After my speech, Pastor Clonch addressed the audience:

We gather here today to lovingly remember and celebrate the life of Larry Smestad. His life was sadly cut short by this serious illness. He fought a good fight.

Chapter 40 Memorial Service

As Tammy and others were sharing today, you have so many memories of Larry's life. It is good to hold on to those memories. Larry, throughout his life's journey, was a good companion to his wife. A friend to all he met—caring, generous, loyal, and thoughtful. He remembered his promises, and he stuck by those whom he loved. May you find comfort and hope in God's promises today that reveal to us the knowledge of the resurrection of Jesus Christ, making it possible for the dead in Christ to live again.

I am reminded of the words of Christ in John 14 where it says, "Let not your hearts be troubled. You believe in God believe also in me. In my father's house are many mansions. If it were not so I would have told you. I go to prepare a place for you. And if I go and prepare a place for you I will come again and receive you to myself that where I am there you may be also."

Remember the times when you have visited family you haven't seen for a long time—the excitement of the journey, the anticipation of reunion. The good feelings you have of knowing that they are preparing to receive you. Our journey here is just for a short time. So spend your time on the important things that matter with God, and family, and friends.

Jesus remembers us when we are alive and when we pass under the valley of the shadow of death. If He goes through all that trouble to prepare a place for us, then it shouldn't surprise us to know that He will come back to take us home because He made us and He wants us to be with Him for eternity.

September of last year, when visiting with Larry and Tammy, Larry was in a hospital bed. Although he was weak and tired at the time, Larry was positive and upbeat. It blew me away. Larry was determined to fight his cancer by going to an alternative treatment center at Uchee Pines in Alabama where they learned a lot of techniques of healthful living, believing the natural way of dealing with his cancer would at least help him to live longer than what the doctors said he would have had with chemotherapy or other treatments.

They were both determined to travel and live life while they had the chance. Buying a motor home, they made many caring friends along the way as I read on Caring Bridge. As they traveled and shared, Tammy shared how to live a healthier lifestyle and Larry shared his story. His passion was to tell everyone to get a colon cancer test. I remember that because I went ahead last fall to have my done, and Larry said, "Good! Good!" He said it as if he was glad to get back at the enemy.

Paul says, "I don't want you to be ignorant brothers and sisters concerning those who fall asleep in Jesus lest you sorrow as others who have no hope. For if we believe that Jesus died and he rose again even so God will bring with them those who sleep in Jesus. For the Lord himself will descend from heaven with a shout with the voice of the archangel, with the trumpet of God, and the dead in Christ shall rise first and then we who are alive and remain shall be caught up together with him in the clouds and meet the Lord in the air, and so shall we ever be with the Lord." And, that's the point! Jesus wants to meet with us, and He wants you to meet with all those who have died.

So this is not the end. It's just a beginning to know that there is a future life, if you really want that life. God will give great honor to the dead by raising them first. He wants those who are alive to witness the fact that He isn't going to forget the dead. We will rejoice as we see them rise and then we will join with them in an eternal embrace because we will never part again. We will always be with the Lord and with each other. And then we'll know that God has fulfilled His promises to us for sure and Larry wants to fulfill His promise to you, too!

What a wonderful day when we get to heaven. He'll wipe every tear from your eyes. There will be no more death nor crying nor pain for the old order of things has passed away. And you can plan on being there too by just accepting Jesus, God's gift of salvation, being sorry for your sins, the things that keep us away from Him, and asking Him, "Lord, I want to be close to You. I want You to live in my life from now on."

In heaven it won't take us long to find Larry. He'll probably be doing something interesting. Working on his house or fiddling with something, or maybe going on a trip somewhere, and he wants to invite you to come with him. But mostly, I think at the very beginning, he'll be waiting right there at the city gate for you. Because he'll remember that he wants to keep his promise to you.

At this time we're going to see some pictures of Larry's life journey and then at the conclusion have a closing prayer. So please, look at these pictures and think of the memories you've had, that you shared together with Larry.

The Gaither Vocal Band sings an unbelievable version of the song "Jesus Loves Me." Larry loved this song, so it was the first song playing on his life journey DVD while pictures scrolled by of Larry as a baby progressing into his adult life. I had found Larry's handwriting on the back of

Chapter 40 Memorial Service

an old picture. Larry had written, "To the best family a person could ask for. Love you all, Larry." I decided to include this on the DVD, knowing it would mean a lot to his family.

Hearing Larry's voice, at times, throughout the DVD was emotional and touching. While drinking water out of a mason jar, Larry said, "Ahh ... water does a body good." While enjoying a meal, Larry said, "I've got to finish what I've got before I eat more." When Larry shared his testimony in Florida, there was a screen directly behind where he stood that said, "Diagnosed with Stage IV Cancer and Faced with Decisions." Larry referred to his conversation with his doctor when he said, "So, how long do I have left?"

Josh Groban's song "You Raise Me Up" softly played throughout Larry's travels and cancer journey. The DVD showed Larry riding his motorcycle, driving the motor home, and holding hands with me while walking the beach. Larry was parasailing and riding the zip line. Larry's hand crossed accomplished tasks off the bucket list.

At the end of the DVD, Tyler surprised me and everyone else with a montage of Larry's life. The flashback included family singing happy birthday, Larry admiring his Corvette, Larry bowling, laughing, honking the horn in the RV, waving while walking on the beach, and riding off in the distance on his motorcycle. As hard as it was to watch, I loved the footage of Larry and me dressed up for dinner walking down the staircase on the Hawaiian cruise ship. The last clip was at Larry's FedEx benefit. Holding the microphone, Larry said, "I miss you guys. Thanks!"

Immediately after the memorial service, ladies from the Champaign Seventh-day Adventist Church served a meal they had prepared for the family. I appreciated the generosity extended by thoughtful people like them.

Larry had a large collection of Harley t-shirts, and I hoped to give these to family members. I brought them along to pass out after dinner. Though many family members had already left, I captured a photo with eight of Larry's family members proudly wearing his Harley t-shirts.

Back row (left to right): Chris Scott, Travis Kern, Mike Kern, Trent Rader, Mike Rader.

Front row (left to right): Tristan Thomas, Heather Scott, Paul Maher.

Chapter 41

"Caring Bridge" Comments

After the service, family and friends posted comments on Caring Bridge. I truly enjoyed reading these comments. It was a pleasure for me to continue learning new things about Larry. The following are a few of the postings:

Tiit Lukk wrote:

"Dear Tammy and family,
The memorial was a true blessing to everyone attending, me included. I think Larry would be very proud. I really feel like if there was someone attending the ceremony who didn't know him very well before got to know him really well by the end of it. We'll all be missing that smile. Our thoughts and prayers are with you!"

Lisa Helgesen wrote:

"Tammy, you and Tyler both touched many hearts yesterday. Larry would have been so proud!"

Laura Miller wrote:

"Love you, Aunt Tammy! You did such a great job Sunday! I am so glad that my uncle had you and your boys in his life. You are very special to our family, and we love you so much. Thank you so much for taking such good care of him."

Randall Lemmon wrote:

"I met Larry nearly 20 years ago in Gibson City. I was delivering for UPS, and he helped me out a lot with directions and such. We passed one another several times a day, and he would always wave and give me that reassuring smile. Larry would always open doors for me and wanted to know how I was doing. Larry was there for me when I lost my wife to scleroderma about 14 years ago. Larry was a true friend, and I will miss him dearly. It was a blessing to go to the funeral yesterday. It really lifted my spirits. I am happy knowing I will see Larry again."

Chapter 42

A New Normal

Grieving was hard work. There was nothing I could do to escape my loss. I felt Larry's absence at all times, in all places. In my journaling, I compared the loss to an empty chair. At home, church, or in public, there was always an empty seat beside me. The empty chair was a constant reminder.

After the service, I spent three long, rough days on my couch. I barely had the energy to eat, drink, or bathe. I was exhausted, unmotivated, and heartbroken. Crying further added to my fatigue. I could not control the tears, nor did I want to. I realized it was healing to cry when I needed to cry. I had been a wife and a caretaker. *Now, where am I to go and what am I to do?* I asked myself.

I received many sympathy cards in the mail, and I appreciated every one of them. But the cards in which the sender took the time to write a personal message meant the most. A church member, Bob Chesnut, understood the importance of sharing the right words at the right time. I am thankful Bob and others took the time to share from their hearts. On Caring Bridge, Bob wrote:

> I hope everyone doesn't forget you just because the memorial service is finished. People don't always understand the impact of this

kind of tragedy. It lasts longer than you might expect, and you will never really be the same again. You have to find a "new normal." So we will pray for you.

Bob understood my pain and my sorrow. He was right. Losing Larry was a tragedy, and I would never really be the same. I knew I had hard days ahead of me rebuilding my life, and I appreciated his prayers.

> *Losing Larry was a tragedy, and I would never really be the same.*

I couldn't anticipate everything that lay ahead, but I chose to face my grief head on. I didn't deny it, and I didn't bury it. I wanted to make Larry proud, honor his memory, and live a life pleasing to God. I made the decision to leave my house every day to visit someone or to do something useful. This would be a first step.

At some point, my mother-in-law, Lois Smestad, shared with me her desire to have the interior of her house painted. I thought this would be a good time for me to tackle the project, and I was glad she accepted my offer. It was a big job to paint all the walls and trim, but it felt good to do something useful for someone else. It was therapeutic for me.

On Tuesday, July 19, 2011, I attended my first hospice sponsored grief support group, *Life After Loss*. Mom Smestad agreed to go with me, and I was glad she did. On the first night it was hard to see and hear so much pain in one room. Cheryl Peterson-Karlan, hospice chaplain, bereavement coordinator, and meeting facilitator, asked each participant to state their name, the name of their deceased loved one, their relationship with that person, and the date of the death. Many individuals were unable to speak, but I pushed myself to do so. Stating Larry's name and the date of his death helped me acknowledge my loss, even though that was hard to do. But this was another important step in my grieving process.

Cheryl and Elizabeth both knew of my intentions to become a hospice volunteer. Cheryl said I needed to participate in the eight-week grief support group before receiving formal training. Since the *Life After Loss* group included over fifteen participants, Cheryl decided to divide the group by offering an afternoon session and an evening session. Since I was not working at the time, I signed up to attend the afternoon class, allowing working participants to attend the evening session. I was honored when Cheryl asked me to attend both sessions. She said, "I think

Chapter 42 A New Normal

you have a lot to offer, and it would be beneficial for you to attend both sessions." I accepted.

I no longer needed the Corvette and decided I would like to find a good home for it. I remembered Gary Linstrom had often talked with Larry about his love of cars and was planning to buy a Corvette when he retired. I called Gary and proceeded to ask if he was interested in purchasing the Corvette at a reasonable price. After discussing this with his wife, he gladly accepted my offer. I was grateful that I was able to pass the keys of this beautiful classic to Larry's good friend who had been so good to us on so many occasions.

I knew it would be hard to clean out the motor home, but I needed to do it. July 25, 2011, was a very emotional day for me. I brought home clothes, kitchen items, and lots of paperwork that had been left behind. The car was full, and I decided to bring in a few items at a time, allowing myself to either dispose of the item or find a place for it. Many things were stored in the motor home and it seemed overwhelming to combine two homes again. I brought in all the paperwork first and came across several cards that Larry had given me for my birthday and Valentine's Day. In the Valentine's Day card, I didn't remember what he had written. As I reread it, the meaning was more powerful now than the first time. Larry wrote, "Thanks for saying I do! I love you, Tammy."

Larry had a Bible in the house but he also kept one in the motor home. Unlike me, he usually kept no extra papers or bulletins in his Bible. Regardless, I felt compelled to open his Bible to see if anything was left behind. And I was glad I did! I found two pieces of paper with Larry's handwriting on them. On one of the papers, Larry wrote, "Five Things to Be Sure You Are Saved":

1. The Holy Spirit should initiate your salvation. John 16:7, John 3:6

2. Realize you are lost. Romans 3:23, Ephesians 2:18

3. Faith

4. Without repentance there is no salvation. 2 Corinthians 7:10

5. Realize you are forgiven. Not guilty! Acts 5:31, Acts 10:43

Larry had many sleepless nights. I think he probably did this study during that time. These words affirmed Larry's close relationship with the Lord.

On the other sheet of paper Larry had written twenty, short inspirational quotes. I had no idea where they came from, but they were typical of Larry's positive, upbeat attitude. Larry wrote:

> Love is a flower, friendship a sheltering tree
>
> Nothing is as strong as gentleness or as gentle as strength
>
> Whatever you give will find countless ways back to you
>
> You are the star for which all evenings wait
>
> The reward for a good deed is to have done it
>
> Time flies ... spend it with people who mean the most to you
>
> The heart has reasons for which reason does not know
>
> To accomplish great things one must not only act, but dream
>
> Take time to laugh, it's the music of the soul
>
> The best ideas come after you think you've run out of them
>
> Promise yourself more moments like this
>
> You worked hard—promise yourself a reward
>
> One little smile can fill the room with sunshine
>
> If you live the present every moment is a new beginning
>
> Music touches feelings that words cannot
>
> Push yourself to notice the extraordinary in the ordinary
>
> Climb high, climb far; your goal the sky, your aim the stars
>
> Footprints on the sands of time are made not by sitting down
>
> Friendship is the gold thread that ties hearts together
>
> Every cloud doesn't mean a storm

I couldn't keep these sayings to myself. I wanted Larry's family and friends to enjoy the gift of hope and inspiration he left behind, so I posted them on Caring Bridge. I decided I would honor Larry's memory by framing copies of his handwritten quotes in a double 5x7-inch frame for Christmas presents.

Chapter 43

Hope and Healing

  Unlike others in my class, I looked forward to attending the grief support group. I processed my thoughts and acknowledged my pain. I wanted each day to get better than the day before. I listened to my inner voice and expressed my feelings. I enjoyed reading Dr. Alan Wolfelt's book *Understanding Your Grief*, which was a gift from hospice. The book focused on ten essential touchstones for finding hope and healing. His advice on setting an intention to heal, exploring feelings of loss, and understanding the six needs of mourning were very beneficial.

  In addition to the weekly reading, I was encouraged to express myself in a corresponding grief journal. As much as I enjoy writing and processing my thoughts through words, I found some of the questions difficult to answer. One of the hardest assignments was to write a letter to the person who died and tell him or her what is in your head and on your heart. I wrote:

  Dear Larry,

    I miss you so much. You were my companion, my friend, and my love. You were gone so quickly, and I am so sorry I didn't get to say goodbye. On Wednesday morning when we hugged I started crying and I didn't say all the things I wanted to tell you. I know that you know I loved you, but I wanted to hold you and have you hear it when you passed away. I am now looking forward to heaven more than ever before. I will see you again, and we will have no more pain or sorrow, thanks to Jesus.

I am doing things daily and weekly that would make you proud. Thank you for making me more confident about myself. As I told you before, I am a better person today after being with you. You brought out the best in me and encouraged me to follow my dreams and talents. I know you would be surprised and honored about your memorial service. Tyler's speech was emotional and heartfelt. Not only did you change me, but you influenced the boys more than you realized. I am also spending as much time as I can with your family.

In closing, I want you to know I will never forget you. You will always be a part of me. Thank you so much for taking good care of me and for loving me. My time on this earth will be short, so I will enjoy life as you would want me to, but I will always look forward to seeing you again.

Love,
Tammy

I am a different person now.

I am a different person now. Different than I was prior to Larry's death. I have loved, lost, and learned. Lord willing, through prayers, I will continue to grow. The most important lessons I have learned throughout my journey are:

- Appreciate today and make it count. I am not guaranteed tomorrow.

- This world is not my home. I am just passing through, so don't get too comfortable here.

- In all circumstances, praise God.

- Love hurts and love heals, but it is always best to choose love.

- Trust in the Lord always. Never lean on my own understanding.

- Seek the Lord. Pray at all times in all circumstances, share joys and sorrows.

- With the Lord leading, embrace challenges and opportunities.

- Never let fear hold me back. God has plans for me. Claim Jeremiah 29:11.

- Throughout life, I will travel through valleys. Rely on God to lead me to safer, higher ground. Reflect on His faithfulness in the past.

- Cherish friends and family. Spend time with them. They are God's gift to you as you are to them.

A Message from the Author:

I may be reached at
www.facebook.com/whynotmebytammycranston.

I welcome comments, questions,
and personal grief stories.

Collectively, we can encourage one another.

We invite you to view the complete
selection of titles we publish at:

www.TEACHServices.com

Scan with your mobile
device to go directly
to our website.

Please write or email us your praises, reactions, or
thoughts about this or any other book we publish at:

www.TEACHServices.com • (800) 367-1844

P.O. Box 954
Ringgold, GA 30736

info@TEACHServices.com

TEACH Services, Inc., titles may be purchased in bulk for
educational, business, fund-raising, or sales promotional use.
For information, please e-mail:

BulkSales@TEACHServices.com

Finally, if you are interested in seeing
your own book in print, please contact us at

publishing@TEACHServices.com

We would be happy to review your manuscript for free.

www.ingramcontent.com/pod-product-compliance
Lightning Source LLC
Chambersburg PA
CBHW081354230426
43667CB00017B/2829